not

so

secret

Imagine what it is like being a cross-cultural missionary – the embarrassing early days when you are learning the language and can't work out what it is you want to buy in the shops and you don't have the words to apologize to your neighbour when your toilet overflows into the flat below. Then later on, you have to try to understand how to function as a church in a society with very different social conventions, work patterns and religious background from everything you have ever known before. Then again, perhaps we don't need to imagine what it is like to physically cross cultures. There are many cultural difficulties and barriers associated with sharing the gospel in post-Christian Britain; it's just that they are so familiar that we don't always recognize them.

In *Not So Secret*, Graham Orr, a long-term missionary in Japan, shares his experience of making friends, building community and sharing the love of Christ in a situation which is very different from the north of England where he grew up. But this isn't just another book of encouraging and amusing missionary stories (though it is that). Using his experiences in Japan as a starting point and reflecting on Scripture and on time spent in the UK church, Orr encourages us to rethink how we can live as missionary Christians in our own culture. This is a challenging, thought-provoking and ultimately heart-warming book. There is a lot of talk in missionary circles about being a 'reflective practitioner'. If you want to know what that means, read this book; you won't find many better examples.

Eddie Arthur, Executive Director, Wycliffe Bible Translators

Are you a Christian who switches off when someone talks about evangelism? It's not your gift, you are too busy and your friends are not interested? Then this charming book is for you. Packed with stories marked by deep humility, this is an account of how a missionary couple stumbled through their early days in Tokyo and came to realize that God could use them without their even knowing it. Their self-deprecating surprise to find how God had worked through – and despite – them is such a refreshing contrast to the brash, upfront evangelist. Brilliant at getting into the culture of others, it offers profound insights from Japan – and

Northern Ireland – which are highly relevant in our postmodern scene. This is a book to buy and give to others – it is so fresh and helpful.

Canon Dr Michael Green, author and speaker

We are often told we need to approach the UK as a mission field. But often those voices make evangelism in a post-Christian culture seem even more difficult, and we are put off. Graham's short book changes all that. Drawing on his long and fruitful ministry in Tokyo, he shows us how, and makes us feel we can do it too. Lively, realistic, easy to read and Christ-centred, this may be the new *Out of the Saltshaker* for our cultural moment.

Julian Hardyman, Senior Pastor, Eden Baptist Church, Cambridge

Three things hinder the witness of many Christians: a belief that it is a task for professionals, a lack of belief that God is in control, and a failure to relate and listen to people before sharing the gospel with them. In this book, Graham Orr draws together his experiences in Japan and the UK, with insights into the Gospel stories, to give a challenge to Christians to realize the joy of being part of a chain that God uses to bring people to know himself. *Not So Secret* is an antithesis and antidote to evangelism manuals, as it calls readers just to live an authentic Christian life, engaging naturally with people they meet, with the conviction that God knows how to bring people to faith in himself. This is a book that will help every Christian to have a useful daily witness to Christ.

Ray Porter, Director of World Mission Studies, Oak Hill College ivp

not so secret

Being contemporary agents for mission

Graham Orr

INTER-VARSITY PRESS
Norton Street, Nottingham NG7 3HR England
Email: ivp@ivpbooks.com
Website: www.ivpbooks.com

First published 2012

British Library Cataloguing in Publication Data
A catalogue record for this book is available from the British Library.

ISBN: 978–1–84474–591–3

Set in Dante 12/15pt
Typeset in Great Britain by CRB Associates, Potterhanworth, Lincolnshire
Printed in Great Britain by the MPG Books Group

*Inter-Varsity Press publishes Christian books that are true to the Bible and that
communicate the gospel, develop discipleship and strengthen the church for its
mission in the world.*

*Inter-Varsity Press is closely linked with the Universities and Colleges Christian
Fellowship, a student movement connecting Christian Unions in universities and
colleges throughout Great Britain, and a member movement of the International
Fellowship of Evangelical Students. Website: www.uccf.org.uk*

contents

acknowledgments

I thank God for Eric, Jane, Pam and Michael through whom he brought me to faith in Christ.

I would like to express my sincere gratitude to the members, past and present, of OMF The Chapel of Adoration for the many lessons God taught me through them, and for their kindness in allowing me to share some of their stories with readers.

Thank you, Marylyn, for encouraging me that I could write. Thanks, Wendy, for intervening to restart the project. Ramon, your hands-on help with proposals to publishers was timely. Sam from IVP, your advice hugely improved the content and readability. My grateful thanks to you all.

A final thanks to Martin Goldsmith for being in on the genesis of the book, for his stimulation and encouragement to keep going, for offering to write the foreword and for being such a special friend and companion on the Jesus Way.

foreword

Having taught and tutored Graham Orr at All Nations Christian College, it was a special pleasure to spend time with him in Tokyo. As we strolled round the ruins of the huge old fortress where the brilliant Jesuit Valignano witnessed to Jesus Christ 400 years ago, we not only talked about those early Jesuit workers in Japan. Graham also shared how he was now learning classical Japanese and reading Kitamori's *A Theology of the Pain of God* which is still so apposite for Japanese Christians – every Japanese student I have tutored has said to me after reading it, 'This is just what we need in Japan.' Graham shared with me some of his perceptive and sensitive insights into contemporary witness in Tokyo, which opened my eyes to much that I had observed during my visit.

The British church has served for centuries in a largely Christian context and has inevitably developed a basically pastoral ministry, teaching and caring for its people. But now we live in a pluralistic and secular society where Christians form a small minority of the population. In the past we may have had ninety-nine sheep safely in the sheepfold and only one lost on the mountains, but today the shepherd with the six sheep within the sheepfold is challenged to reach the ninety-four lost sheep. How can we adapt our churches to make them into mission churches rather than just feeding the few sheep we still have?

In its history over the centuries the church in Japan has sometimes had to suffer even martyrdom and has always been a small minority of its people. It has grown up with the task of mission and evangelism within the challenging context of their own strongly non-Christian and pluralistic culture. They have therefore so much to teach us. And we are reminded of Paul's picture of the church worldwide, in which no member dares to say, 'We don't need you' (see 1 Corinthians 12:21). The British and Japanese churches have much to give each other in our mission calling.

Today in Britain, as indeed in virtually all countries, we live in a globalized world. Our mission and evangelism must relate to this multi-ethnic and multicultural context. This book with its Japanese and British background will help us rethink the good news of Jesus and how we can live it and witness to it verbally in this relatively new situation. Cross-cultural mission relates not only to inter-ethnic approaches, but also to inter-generational communication. Grandparents' culture differs radically from that of their grandchildren! And considerable cultural adaptation is needed both by our churches and by Christians individually when crossing the borders between different educational and class backgrounds.

After some twenty years in Japan Graham has penetrated into the worldview and thinking of ordinary Japanese. He understands how they feel. Added to his evident personal sensitivity and his deeply biblical spirituality, he applies his Tokyo experience to issues related to our witness in Northern Ireland where he has his home and to Britain more widely.

I am confident that readers of this very practical, spiritual and insightful book will find it a real help in their own walk with the Lord in the midst of a sadly non-Christian society. It will help us to witness more relevantly, more lovingly and with greater cultural awareness.

Martin Goldsmith
All Nations Christian College
Ware, England

introduction

What would a new work colleague think if you mentioned to them you were a Christian? What would your neighbours say if you asked them to study the Bible with you? How would a close friend react if you invited them to your church? How would you feel making any of these offers?

Christianity magazine's 'The Evangelism Issue', in July 2011, began with the statement, 'The UK is not an easy place to convince people to be Christians. People are often suspicious, angry or politely disinterested when discussing faith.'

Would your work colleagues think it strange you were a Christian? Would your neighbours be suspicious of your offer to study the Bible? Would they suspect an ulterior motive? Would your close friends react strongly to an invitation to church? Or would they just dismiss it with disdain? How would you feel if they did?

Do you ever wonder, 'How can I tell others about Jesus in a way that works?' *Christianity*'s editorial summed up evangelism in the UK: 'There doesn't seem to be a lot of consensus on how to do it, or even what message we should be presenting.'

I have spent half my adult life working and worshipping in the UK, and half working and worshipping in Japan. I have seen this confusion in both places.

Returning from Japan to the UK for one year in five, I have seen huge changes in UK culture. It is ethnically diverse. There are many different views about life. It is postmodern. Many views, complementary and conflicting, happily coexist. No-one is considered 'right'. It is largely post-Christian. Many people feel they can dismiss the Christian faith. These shifts in attitude over recent decades characterize many English-speaking countries around the world, leaving Christians wondering what to do.

I cannot tell people in Japan about Jesus in the same way as I would if I were in the UK. Conversely, in the light of these recent cultural changes in our home countries, how do we tell people about Jesus at home, now it has changed so much?

We all seem to agree something should be done: '90% of us think seeing people become Christians is of central import-ance. Where we fall down is actually getting out there and doing it.'[1] I have tried getting out there and doing it in Japan. It has meant learning a new language and adapting to a new culture. It has also meant making mistakes and learning (often reluctantly) new lessons about how God is at work in his world; lessons that I trust will help you in telling others about Jesus in ethnically diverse, postmodern and post-Christian settings like the UK.

If you feel awkward or uncomfortable inviting others to learn more about Jesus, that's OK. I feel the same. But God is remarkably untroubled by our ineptitude. He continues to draw men and women to trust in Jesus as their sole hope and Saviour. How he has done that in my life, how he did that in your life, and how he will do that in the lives of your neigh-bours, colleagues and friends – that is the vibrant dynamic of mission.

I am convinced that God is at work in our world. I see him at work in two primary ways: he is at work in those of us who already know him and he is at work in others around us who do not yet know him. It is when these two arenas of God's activity overlap that we witness real mission. We are invited, even called, to participate in God's mission to God's world. It is a daunting task because we don't always know how to respond.

The most important thing for you to do as you read is to pray. Ask God the Holy Spirit to show you how he is at work in your life and in the lives of others around you. You may be surprised. This is a short book – don't read it too quickly. Ponder as you read. Catch a glimpse of what God is doing. He is at work in you and through you. It may be to allay a neighbour's suspicion of Christians. It may be to counter a colleague's aversion to Christianity. It may be to attract a close friend presently dis-interested in Jesus. It may be all of these things as you relate to different people.

God's kingdom continues to come. It comes as we each 'go and make disciples of all nations' (Matthew 28:19). It still happens today, even in unlikely places, through unlikely people like you and me.

God has chosen each of us to be a not-so-secret agent in his mission to the world.

beginning together

Toilet training

It was blocked. We were living in an upstairs flat of shaky wooden construction in the north-east of Sapporo, the main city in Japan's northernmost island of Hokkaido. The toilet was blocked. I flushed it again to clear the blockage. The toilet bowl filled nicely, then overflowed, tipping not-at-all-clear water all over the floor. It leaked through the floor and, unseen by me, dripped from the ceiling of the flat below. The Japanese tenants below would find toilet overflow dripping into their house unpleasant enough, but ours was worse: it was foreigners' toilet waste.

We hadn't been at language school many months. I had lived in Japan for a while before getting married, so I was a few lessons ahead of my wife Alison. But I hadn't yet reached a chapter on apologies deep enough for this level of disaster.

The toilet bowl was still full, so I rang the experienced missionary who looked after the first-term missionaries. She came and apologized for the foreigners upstairs who had flushed their toilet contents down the walls. Even now I cannot begin to figure out what she must have said to them. In the nine months we lived in that apartment, we did not have any lengthy conversation with those neighbours. They probably didn't want to have one with us.

Do you feel unsettled about telling others about Jesus? I expect so. Do you feel tongue-tied, embarrassed, unsure? Probably. I know I do. Do you run through mental menus of what points you should try to get across, or worry about not having an answer if they ask 'that' question? That is normal. It is usual. It is where we all live. Yet despite our feelings of inadequacy, God so often uses us anyway.

After Japanese language school, we were sent to a church in Tokyo for training. I was the fifth member of the pastoral staff. When I was alone in the church office and the telephone rang, I would panic. I could say, 'Hello' and '*Hai, hai*' throughout the conversation, and even finish it off with a correctly pronounced 'Thank you', but I rarely understood much of the content. After eighteen months of feeling inadequate, we packed up to return to the UK for a year. As we moved out, I gave a book to a woman in the neighbourhood who used to smile at me as I walked past her house on my way to work. I had imbibed enough Japanese culture simply to thank her for her polite kindness and leave her a small present.

Years later, I heard that this had led to her conversion and that she was now leading a church housegroup in that local area.

With a one-year-old to look after, my wife hadn't been able to work on the staff team and felt even less involved than I did. Some Friday evenings, a local Christian nurse used to come round, do a jigsaw puzzle with Alison and try out her English conversation. We were the first missionaries she had ever met.

Years later, she recalled that her clearest impression had been that missionaries were just ordinary people – like her. She is now a missionary herself, working as a nurse in an Asian country closed to traditional missionary work. We'll hear more of her story later. All we ever did with her was jigsaws. But God used our small, seemingly insignificant contribution as part of his larger plan.

New opportunities

It was probably just another sunny day in northern Palestine, as two brothers sat cross-legged in their father's boat at the lakeside harbour and dragged the nets over one by one, examined them for tears and holes and, with robust needles, set about mending the fraying fabric. They talked and chatted with each other about fish, the weather, their kids, their wives, the village. The simple gossip of life. Two other brothers pushed their boat off into the blue water and, with practised hand, cast their circular nets into the lake.

Jesus had seen them around plenty of times. From time to time, he'd struck up conversation with them, sometimes they with him. They were just normal local men. But that morning Jesus ended his conversation with a carefully thought-out offer: 'Come, follow me and I will make you fishers of men' (Matthew 4:19; Mark 1:17).

Peter and Andrew, James and John must have been intrigued. I am sure they were curious. I do not know whether it was the note of invitation or the tone of command that drew them in. I wonder whether they felt adventurous or afraid. Probably both. They left their boats full of fish, their nets full of holes and everything else with Zebedee, the father of James and John, and took the walk of a lifetime along the lakeshore with Jesus.

I would like to know what they talked about that day. I would like to know what Jesus said to them about being fishers of men. What questions did they ask? What answers did he give? What questions would I have asked? What questions would you have asked?

All I know is that, early in their time with Jesus, the disciples were often confused. It seems they didn't quite know what they were supposed to be doing, or how they were to do it. That first walk along the lakeside with Jesus was introductory. It doesn't seem to have included a detailed presentation on missionary strategy. In those early weeks and months, it doesn't seem that Jesus explained all they were to do and how they were to do it. If he had, they probably wouldn't have been able to take it in. Jesus welcomed them to join him in his task, and let them find out the nature of their own individual contributions as things went along. So if you are unsure of how to tell others about Jesus, that's not unusual; it is normal. Jesus will teach us as we go along.

Our contribution: insignificant or unique?

I had just finished teaching a group of seven or eight women about daily devotional Bible reading, the dynamics of fellowship in small groups and the seeds of some of my thoughts on evangelism. As we chatted together afterwards, the most mature Christian in the group admitted that she always felt guilty for not speaking to others about Jesus. She felt she was no good at evangelism and was ashamed of not having brought her friends to church. All I could tell her was that I had felt the same, even as a missionary, for many years. I don't have the 'missionary spirit' I see in others who talk to people on trains, invite their neighbours to church and have evangelistic meetings in their homes. I don't feel it is my style.

Although these activities can of course be part of local mission, I had begun to think they were neither the only, nor necessarily the most important, activities in evangelism.

There have been plenty of days when I have felt there was little or nothing I could do. But then I have to remember that the task is not all mine. God is at work through many others, even in a country like Japan where the 'salt content', the number of Christians, is well below 1%. Here in the UK, the percentage of Christians may be ten to fifteen times higher, but both in Japan and here I have often felt useless when trying to tell people about Jesus, and I have had to remember that Jesus chose me, and not the other way around, so everything is not dependent on my (dis)ability.

As I have reflected on my own feelings of helplessness in the face of the enormity of the task, the weakness of my desire to make Jesus known – which may seem strange given that I am a missionary – and my frustration in failing to do it well, I have discovered afresh the variety of roles that I, others and God play in telling people about Jesus. There are times when I may consider my role small, even insignificant. Nevertheless, I take courage precisely because it is 'my' contribution. It is one that God wishes and chooses to make through me. I understand that I can do nothing of myself, as Jesus himself told us, in the context of mission: 'Apart from me you can do nothing' (John 15:5). But it is here that I find my own unique role, because, like Peter and Andrew, I also hear Jesus say to me, 'I chose . . . and appointed you to go and bear fruit.' God has chosen me, and you, to 'bear fruit – fruit that will last' (John 15:16). We could debate whether the context of the Upper Room discourse in John 15 requires that this fruit be interpreted as one of personal character formation or of disciple-making. But, as I hope we shall see together, these two areas are intertwined twin fruits of the same vine. Both are integral to the being and doing of local mission.

Of all the people I baptized during the twelve years I was leading the church, The Chapel of Adoration in Tokyo, I think there was only one person for whom my own contribution could be considered major – and she was my daughter. For the others, my own part was probably quite small. In the stories they told in baptism interviews as testimony to how God had fished them out of the water, my beginners' Bible studies and sermons were rarely mentioned. I am glad to know it doesn't all depend on me, but on God who initiates and oversees the entire process.

They spoke of the way God used words spoken by Christian teachers, care given by Christian neighbours, love expressed through a smile and a welcome in another church, and many other ways. We will touch on these in the following pages. As I stood with each person in the baptismal pool, I took great joy from seeing how God had shepherded them through so many small contributions, including mine, to the point of repentance and confession of faith in Jesus.

Everyday opportunities

However, as the disciples found, in the rough and tumble of ordinary life, on roads, in boats, in religious meetings or in people's homes, discerning our own contribution takes some practice, in knowing ourselves, in knowing others and in knowing God. Let me tell you a little about myself. I like board games, table tennis, snooker and science fiction. I play the piano accordion and chromatic harmonica. I have written a few songs. I jog a little, not for pleasure. I can juggle. I enjoyed acting but never get the chance nowadays. I have done origami since I was eleven. I like rearranging the furniture (more tricky than it sounds in a 550-square-foot flat for four). I have begun reading poetry. This is me. Quirky, you may say, but me.

Let me ask you a few questions to get you started. What are your hobbies? What do you enjoy doing? Our hobbies are a personal, uniquely flavoured part of our lives. I, for instance, learned to juggle while at university (instead of revising!). When I was teaching at a secondary school in Oxford, I started an after-school juggling club. Around eight or ten boys came once a week, and I taught them to juggle. A couple of years later, I popped into a Christian bookshop in Oxford and was greeted with 'Good morning, Mr Orr' from the young man behind the counter. I only half-recognized him and had no idea of his name. He was one of those juggling club students. He explained that some things I had said had really made him think. He had then begun to attend a local church, where he became a Christian, and now he was leading worship in his church. I can't remember saying anything meaningful to any of the boys during the club meetings. But God obviously had been at work, without me knowing.

Where do you work? Most people don't work where you do. The fact that you work there, not somewhere else, is not arbitrary. It is your unique location. Who do you come into contact with? Don't confine yourself to just your office colleagues. A friend of mine works in a large bookshop in the city. Most days she walks past an older woman sitting on the pavement selling *The Big Issue* magazine. She can see her from the book counter. She often takes a cup of tea out to her. When she heard she had had a baby, she visited her home. Who knows where this may lead? The way we talk and relate in each situation is different according to each person's needs. But we will give more time to this later.

Where do you live? This also is uniquely individual. A young couple in our church have moved recently into a new housing development. The area is reasonably close to their jobs in Belfast. Their relocation was a deliberate choice to live as Christians in that area. The wife told me she wanted to make new friends but felt awkward if the only purpose was to invite them to church. Then she chatted about the young woman she has got to know as she puts out the bins, and how they talk and go for walks together. She was so happy just to have made a real friend. Talking about Jesus and inviting her to church all come later, as we will see. Our initial contribution is small and slow, but it is never insignificant in God's plans.

We need to maintain this perspective, namely that the task is wholly God's, but we are called upon to fulfil a vital, hand-picked role. God has chosen us to be a part of his process of welcoming others into his kingdom. I have a tendency to oscillate between proudly thinking my role is over-important (especially when I come across a method or book that seems to produce results for a while) and, when things don't seem to work, rushing too easily to the opposite conclusion that nothing I do is worthwhile. The corrective to this tendency of mine is to discern more clearly my own role, the role of others and God's role in each relationship I have.

So, as we travel together through the following chapters, my task is to help you become more aware of the opportunities and challenges of being part of God's continuing activity to introduce the billions of people in our world to Jesus, right where you are. It is also to help you to know how to respond appropriately to those challenging opportunities. There are no clever ideas or methods that will work automatically. The task is altogether larger, because it is God's, and altogether more individual, because God has called you to be involved in it. That is why we need a guidebook to the territory to help us find our way.

As I have considered the sprawling mass of individuals called Tokyo, and as you consider the men and women you work with, your neighbours, school friends, university class-mates, those you jog with, go for a drink with, meet at the shops or in the park, your family or occasional strangers who strike up conversation, we discover that each relationship is unique and we have a unique contribution to make to each of their lives. In the overall picture, the one that only God knows (he paints it), our contribution is as necessary as the many others God will make through other people. Like any one piece of a jigsaw puzzle, it is necessary to the completion of the task. As we think these things through together, I pray that God will help you discern the contribution he wishes to make through you to those around you.

The significance of our contribution to world mission, reaching out to the lives of the crowds of needy people around us, is not proportional to our efforts, well-meaning and necessary though they are to the task. It is a direct product of our own deeper appreciation of our human uniqueness, because God has created us all differently. Of course, this rests even more deeply on our own closeness to, and blessedness in, Christ. However, an awareness of the particular person I am, and how Jesus reaches out to others in the crowd through precisely that, fills me with deep-seated joy in life and expect-ation of his activity in me and through me. Without this understanding, my evangelistic attempts become methodical, mechanical, general, superficial, impersonal, irrelevant, unloving, even predatory – all of which will push others away from us, from the church and from Jesus.

Being a pastor of a large church isn't the best job for being able to get to know a lot of non-Christians who have no interest yet in Jesus. I tend to have more contact a lot later on in the process. You, in your job, workplace, family and with friends, probably have far more opportunities, which also count as evangelism but don't fall so easily into the categories we are used to. So enjoy life, your work (there are always some bits we can't enjoy), hobbies and recreation. For it is here that God is at work in us and through us.

Hand-painted artwork

Two Japanese artists, mother and daughter, designed the church in which I served as pastor for twelve years. One of their friends, renowned Japanese artist Kaii Higashiyama, kindly presented the church with two of his own pictures. They have the initials EA at the bottom left-hand corner, which stands for *épreuve d'artiste*, or artist's proof. It indicates that the painting is one of a number (in this case ten) of high-quality copies made from the original painting for the artist's own personal use. We were honoured to have them hanging in the church lounge.

Despite coming into the world uniquely fashioned by the gentle hand of the Creator of Art himself, sadly we each begin our lives unfamiliar with the treasure of our true uniqueness; we miss the signature in the bottom corner of our lives that marks us out as individual, unique creations. We are each far more special than even one of ten copies. We are uniquely handcrafted – all of the millions of Japanese and the millions living in the UK, North America and across the world. As Christians whom Jesus has hand-picked to go and bear fruit, we should thrill even more in the discovery of this uniqueness.

It was just an average morning for Peter and Andrew, James and John, when Jesus happened by with the inviting command: 'Come, be my disciples, and I will show you how to fish for people!' (Matthew 4:19 NLT). The uneducated fishermen became aware of the immensity of the task in bite-sized steps. They came to understand the limits of their human strength, as they travelled with Jesus, saw what he was doing and got involved. They experienced mounting excitement, as Jesus taught, trained and encouraged them in their various contributions.

As we set out together, we remember that God has initiated this process by first graciously calling us to follow him. Jesus took the two pairs of brothers on a lakeside walk, and coaxed these unexpected, unknown, inexperienced men into making their own unique contribution to Jesus' mission.

Jesus, the Son of God, became a man in our world. Eternity himself lived in our small squeeze of time. We read in the Gospels how he transformed the lives of people like Peter and Andrew. We know how he has transformed our own lives, and we long for him to transform the lives of those around us.

We are each born into a journey. God arranges a unique set of parameters that encapsulate our early formation. How God will break in on that journey and reveal his own artistic hand no-one can know. In our own lives, there seemed to be little action for many years. We lived in the dark. We continued in glad ignorance of our uniqueness. But we each have stories of how God met us on the road. As we now look out for others, we must appreciate where they are. Of the billions of people standing on the planet's surface right now, so many live in their own I-don't-know-who-made-me corner. They have never read the Bible. They have never been to a church. They may have never seen a cross. They have not heard the word 'Easter'. They have no Christian friends.

looking around from where you are

Beginning with babies

We had been shopping at the local co-op most days for eighteen months, we were highly visible, white-skinned, blue-eyed, brown-haired foreigners, but no-one had ever spoken to us. We were at language school, and the co-op was a good place to shop because you didn't need much Japanese to buy groceries there.

Yet the first time we went with our newborn baby Kathryn, everyone crowded round to look, poke and gape at our daughter. It was as if we had suddenly graduated as human beings and joined the same world as everyone else. Suddenly we were approachable. Maybe that is what the incarnation is about.

Alison took our son Daniel to kindergarten on the back of her bike. Most children arrived in school buses that ran through their local areas. The few mothers who came by bicycle would drop off their kids and pick them up at the end of the day. One of these mothers, Sachiko, lived near us.

Alison often talked to her while waiting at the school gate. Daniel, aged five and in his last year at the kindergarten, often used to go over to Sachiko's house to play with her three-year-old son.

That year, Alison invited Sachiko to the children's Christmas event at our church. Despite having attended the Christmas service at the kindergarten, which had a Christian foundation and ethos, she was surprised to be invited: 'I'm not a Christian. Is it all right to come?' she asked. She came along and seemed to enjoy it. In April, Daniel began primary school, and we lost touch with Sachiko. Two years later, I was out shopping late one afternoon at one of our local shops, five minutes' walk away, when I bumped into her. Her surprise and joy at seeing me was greater than I expected. As we stood on the pavement, her son perched on the back of her bike, Sachiko explained. She had just received an invitation to our church's Easter event. But not having been in contact for two years, she felt awkward about turning up. Before going out shopping, she had been talking with a friend about coming to the event, and she felt the coincidence of meeting me was a further encouragement to attend. She enjoyed the Easter event and began coming to church every week. She was often the last one to leave on Sunday afternoon, as late as four or five o'clock. She would stay for lunch, as most people did, and then spend the afternoon chatting with others. Her son enjoyed playing with Daniel. She joined the Ladies' Circle, one of our women's groups. Two years later, she asked to be baptized and was quickly accepted. The process had taken five years of contact with us. Then she became a leader of one of those women's groups herself. She understands the dynamics of a journey to Jesus very well. This could have happened anywhere. All Alison did was take her son to school. All I did was go shopping one day.

There are parent-and-toddler groups in many churches in the UK these days. Alison (now with teenage children) goes along to our home-church parent-and-toddler group to talk to the young mothers, grandmothers and childminders. Most are from non-Christian backgrounds. Who knows what God will do?

Many people were involved in the various stages of Sachiko becoming a Christian – some consciously, others unaware of their involvement. Each individual's journey to Jesus is different, but all such journeys are guided by God, who works in unseen and unexpected ways to lead people from darkness to light. How may God be involving you in the lives of those around you? Can you catch a glimpse of where he is already at work? Do not discount any places or people. Pray with anticipation for God to show you where else he is at work.

Look at me, for example

In 2007, I returned to my home town, Hull in East Yorkshire, UK, for the first time in more than twenty years. Driving down suddenly familiar streets was as unsettling as meeting myself coming the other way. I stood in front of the home in which I had grown up, and then walked 500–600 yards along the road to my primary school. This was the only world I knew for eighteen years. My best friend lived in the next street. His father, Eric, ran a youth club at the Methodist church on Friday nights. I often went along to play snooker and table tennis and have cushion fights, before Eric would tell everyone a Bible story. I don't remember any of them. Five or six years later as a sixth former, I had heated discussions with a Christian girl, Jane, expressing my scorn over how ludicrous Christianity and the existence of God were from a scientific viewpoint.

She told me, 'If you want to believe, read the New Testament with an open mind and you'll believe.' I wanted to get the issue sorted out before going to university, so I decided to read the New Testament, not believe, and that would be the end of it. But how could I get my hands on a Bible? I approached my best friend's dad, Eric, and asked if I could borrow one. (How much joy did that give him, I now wonder?) I read the New Testament during the four weeks of sitting my A levels. I understood nothing, except maybe that I should try harder to be a nicer person, and I went off to university with the problem solved.

In the week before term began, I went to a few social events, one of which was a barn dance. I met a nursing student, Pam, who had a Yorkshire accent. Attracted, I struck up a conversation with her. She said, 'I'm a Christian; on Sundays I go to church. Would you like to come?' I had no interest in church, but quite a bit of interest in Pam, so I agreed. I went to church that first Sunday and couldn't find her among all the people – but I did become a Christian that morning.

None of us can tell where our small actions may lead. God uses everyday activities – snooker, school, Yorkshire accents and barn dances – to nudge us along. Neither Eric nor Jane nor Pam knows what I have gone on to do. But I am immensely grateful to God for their contribution to my life.

Can you imagine me? 'He has never been into a church. He doesn't even know where the local churches are, although he has walked past them. He has never read the Bible. There are no Bibles on the bookshelf in his house. He doesn't under-stand that Christmas is about more than presents, or that Easter is about more than chocolate. He doesn't know that Jesus has anything to do with him whatsoever, dead or alive.' Even I find it hard to imagine me!

Can you imagine someone who has never seen a Bible, does not know a Christian, has no idea that the church has any relevance to life? There are almost certainly people near where you live or work who are like that. Indeed, there are millions of such people in the world. In Japan, in Mongolia, in Turkey, in your town or village, whatever continent it may be on, and increasingly in Western countries with a Christian heritage. Many others you know are already slightly further along in their journey to Jesus because they know you are a Christian, whether or not you have talked to them about it.

How can we bridge that initial gap? It may seem impossible. But the answer is more straightforward than we think. God has provided common ground on which each of us can walk to accompany others on their journey to Jesus. For anyone, the process of believing in Jesus, becoming part of the local church and reaching out to others is a long one. We are unlikely to see the whole of any one person's journey. But God wants all of us to play our various parts in many such journeys.

What did Jesus do?

I saw a young woman on a train in Tokyo wearing a WWJD (What Would Jesus Do?) bracelet. A few of her friends had them too. I wondered if they had any idea what the initials stood for. Maybe these bracelets have become a new unthinking fashion. Maybe they were a gift from a well-meaning homestay family in New Zealand or the USA. I do not know. Have they been popular where you live? But when you stop and think about it, what did Jesus do? He stepped across an infinitely huge gap in order to walk with us in our world. When he arrived here, what did Jesus do?

We might conclude that he did surprisingly little. He had been waiting for ever to enter our world as God-become-man, and then, when he finally arrived, it seems he did little of consequence for about 10,000 days. All he did was live. Simply. Quietly. Unobtrusively. Patiently. Obediently. He didn't preach in the synagogue in Nazareth. He didn't heal his younger brothers' cuts and bruises. He didn't hand out Messiah tracts. Actually, we know almost nothing of what Jesus did for those first thirty years of his life.

John and Matthew knew Jesus for a thousand days or so. I do not know how much Jesus told them of his life up to that point, how many stories he shared with them of his growing up and work experiences. Mark and Luke interviewed eye-witnesses and sourced information from family and friends. But between them, they didn't come up with much material from those first thirty years that they could include in an account of his early life. What are we supposed to make of the hidden years in Nazareth? Maybe we should conclude little, since there is so little evidence. We should certainly reject any conclusions that our achievement-obsessed culture might draw about those years being worthless or unsuccessful. We can say that Jesus lived. That was the groundbreaking purpose of the incarnation. He 'became human and lived here on earth among us' (John 1:14 NLT).

Do you sometimes feel there is so much living to do, so many meals to be cooked, emails to write, deadlines to be met, kids to pick up, that there is no time to tell others about Jesus? Such activities, as long as we are not chronically overbusy, are not separate from telling others about Jesus, but an integral part of it. It is in doing these sorts of things that we truly live alongside others.

Jesus filled his own storytelling with countless real-life details and illustrated his teaching with intriguing episodes from everyday life. He may well have had them all thought up before he left heaven, but it seems he took time to relearn them when watching farmers sow seed, men being mugged, Pharisees praying on the corner and sparrows dying. He participated in the world around him. He entered fully into the place where he had been sent, the place chosen for him to grow up in. As the poster says, 'Blossom where you are planted.' As Luke recorded, 'And Jesus grew in wisdom and stature, and in favour with God and men' (Luke 2:52).

What have I done?

For Alison and me, new missionaries with adult bodies but less idea of culture and language than a toddler, we had to acquire the language and to absorb, and be absorbed by, the culture. That meant six to eight hours a day in language classes and private study. But a lot of learning was done outside of such formal periods, simply by having to get on with life, falteringly, uncertainly and hesitantly. We learned how not to fall over on hard-packed icy paths for five months of the year. We figured out how not to let our newborn baby daughter freeze to death overnight (this not by trial and error). Living meant cooking with chopsticks and eating seaweed and dealing with blocked toilets. Maybe one day we might speak to someone about Jesus, but in the meantime we had to live.

Looking back on a decade of leading a Japanese church, I could summarize it thus: thirty-eight baptisms, five weddings, four funerals, 276 sermons, a pastor's ordination and a missionary valedictory service. Many of our cultures, obsessed with achievement, success and 'So what have you done with your life?' questions, would maybe like to know these gaunt statistics. But my life is far more than statistics (even if I was once a maths teacher). Like Paul, I admit I can't always remember who I have baptized, and that these numbers are probably imprecise. But my life cannot be reduced to numbers.

Most of my life and living does not show up on a spreadsheet of success. What is not recorded here is of far greater import.

Even as a missionary, most of my time is not spent telling others about Jesus. Most of my life is about being at work (in my case a church building), being at home with family, and making time to be away from both these places, to be alone and to be refreshed, to try to survive the stress, busyness and fatigue of striving to achieve too much.

Most of our life is spent in the workplace, in the home with family, in recreation and living, and not in telling others about Jesus. Nor should it be, though even the briefest self-examination reveals a teasing guilt that expects it should be. Rather than attempting to locate the source of that guilt, which would require a few more chapters, I would like simply to affirm the value of our everyday living and its foundational role in our task of telling others about Jesus.

Living, plain getting on with life, is a perfect opportunity, matched to each of our unique situations, for us to learn. Much of what we learn, how we struggle and adapt to situations, is common human experience, but as Christians we also gain a unique perspective. Let me illustrate.

One day, Jesus was on a hill teaching a crowd of people about a range of day-to-day issues: divorce, anger, what to wear, not having enough to eat. To show them how to trust God more deeply, he told them, 'Look at the birds of the air . . . See how the lilies of the field grow' (Matthew 6:26, 28). I don't think Jesus explained it this way because he had previously worked it all out as a good sermon illustration, while doing research on how to be a Saviour from the safety of heaven, but because he had spent thirty years in a human body living up-country (Nazareth), where watching birds and looking at flowers were all the entertainment there was. I believe Jesus had enjoyed looking at flowers and birds and, reflecting on their delicate beauty, had come to see them as examples of his own Father's care and provision. It was through his human eyes and human experience that he gained this insight. Even Jesus did not have instant answers, but came to understanding through a process, which he shared with the crowd of people who lived in similar circumstances, with surprisingly similar concerns.

After the day's teaching, Jesus came down from the mountainside and arrived home in Capernaum to be met by a Roman centurion whose servant was at death's door. In the ensuing conversation, again about faith, the centurion exclaims, 'Lord, I do not deserve to have you come under my roof. But just say the word, and my servant will be healed' (Matthew 8:8). There was no precedent for believing this possible. This was not even a man who had spent hours studying the Old Testament. He was a Gentile (a non-Jew) and a soldier, part of a military occupation. The depth of his faith in Jesus came largely from his insights into everyday life: 'For I myself am a man under authority, with soldiers under me. I tell this one, "Go," and he goes; and that one, "Come," and he comes. I say to my servant, "Do this," and he does it' (Matthew 8:9). We too must be open to learn all we can from the exigencies of daily life. In God's hands, these experiences, both painful and joyful, can become authentic stepping stones to someone else's life.

How do you feel about where you live, where you work and what you do? Though your reactions are individual to you, they are also likely to be common to many other people. Your own honest struggles with the dynamics of office relationships, your anxiety over redundancy plans, frustration with noisy neighbours, disappointment over your local club's relegation, these are all common ground with the human experience of hundreds of people. Because we are Christians, there will also be measures of courage amidst struggle, peace in times of anxiety, calm in frustration and hope in times of despair. At some point, these characteristics may be attractive to someone in drawing them to journey to Jesus. However, initially we form relationships through our common, human, rough-and-ready reactions to life.

Where do I begin?

When I first came to Japan, I stayed for ten days with a friend and her parents in a suburb of Yokohama, just south of Tokyo. After a week in the big city, I decided that I didn't like the narrow roads and crowded streets. The urban landscape was too oppressive and threatening. I didn't feel I would ever be able to relax or enjoy living in such an unsettling environment. It has taken maybe ten years, but I have come to appreciate many aspects of life in the megacity. I enjoy the quaint, narrow streets and barely notice the crowds, and I have become used to the bus and train systems, to slow traffic and cyclists riding down the wrong side of the road – occasionally I am one of them. Like any place, some aspects of urban life are good and some are not so good. It is at once an exciting place to live, yet also isolating. It can thrill, but leaves many feeling lonely. I realize I am here at God's bidding, not my own. I live here in response to God's initiative. This is where God has put me, to tell others about Jesus.

My lesson

I took up a musical instrument in my early forties, as a new challenge. Twice a month I travel across Tokyo for a music lesson. The journey is forty-one minutes by train. Even in the afternoon, I usually cannot find a seat. I stand next to the doors and watch the concrete rush past. People get on and off every two or three minutes. Businessmen in suits, office staff, high school boys with deep voices and high, black collars. Obsessive mobile phone users set their thumbs texting within a few seconds of entering the train; others equally swiftly close their eyes and sleep away their tired lives, glad of a few minutes of peace. At busy times, the trains can easily carry 150 people per carriage, but there is likely to be only one Christian in each carriage. Maybe it is me. Of the thousands of middle-sized office blocks I pass crossing the city, few have any Christians at all working in them.

At my destination, twenty train lines disgorge thousands of passengers every few minutes. Over a million people a day pass through the station. I join the flood and head out towards the skyscraper district. For six or seven minutes I thread my way between forty-storeyed, futuristically shaped towers to reach the Sumitomo building, where I slip through the automatic doors into the triangular prism atrium, fifty-two floors high. An elevator effortlessly conveys me to the seventh floor. How many people work in this building? How long would it take me simply to say hello to each one? If there were a thousand people in this building, then I would probably not find many more Christian believers than there are students in our music class of twelve.

If I were to take you to the forty-fifth floor observation deck on the sharply sculptured towers of the Tokyo Metropolitan Government Building, you could scan the Kanto plain, the largest flat area of Japan, and lose your senses in the scale of grey construction, 30 million people within 30 miles.

How do I begin to speak of Jesus, to introduce him to the torrent of human life in Tokyo? I am not allowed to enter any of the other fifty-two office floors in this building. But here I am at my Tuesday music lesson in the Asahi Culture Centre, trying to get to know the eleven other people in my class. This is where I am. I can't play well, and neither can my fellow students. We have that in common. They all live similar distances away and value the friendship and camaraderie of the group. So do I. Since this is a daytime lesson, they are all retired, mostly men. What do I have in common with a seventy-year-old retired Japanese businessman? Many talk of aches and pains, of not being able to do what they used to. I can identify with those feelings. I suffered from chronic fatigue syndrome and was bedridden for a whole year. My constitution is not great. I share their feelings of weakness. So we are friends. I pray they will see Jesus at work in me.

Whatever our culture, language, educational background or standard of living, we have undergone a journey, growing up through adolescent and teenage years, through work experience and life experience. If you are at all like me, it has been the tough times that have taught you most about who you are and how you tick. Though my relationship with Jesus is the most intimate and precious part of my life, in the initial stages of getting to know people, I find it is the tough experiences in life that create common ground.

I still remember my own perplexity when I received this phone call: a forty-two-year-old father of three had been found dead in his bed by his children when they called him for breakfast. The youngest child was only three. The verdict was sudden death by overwork, without any previous symptoms or warning. What did I have to do? I did no more than cry at the funeral. I had received the call from the widow's sister, one of our church members, who had recently begun taking her sister to a church near where the young family lived. The pastor of that church conducted the funeral service. Church members provided meals and looked after the kids. My only contribution was to be there and add my tears. If you had been involved, your contribution would no doubt have been different from mine, something else that was needed.

I presume you are reading this because you also are aware of the immense privilege of being where God has placed you, and are considering your response to similar questions: How do I step out of my home-made security and pass on such good news to the people around me with whom I live and work? You step out into the unknown of other people's lives, but along the path of your own everyday life experience of being the person you are right now.

3:

looking around at others

On your special day

The bride tugged on her father's elbow, and he slowed down. The congregation rose to welcome them with restrained murmurs: 'Look at the dress', 'Isn't she beautiful?' The organ music stopped as they drew level with the front pew. The bridegroom bowed hesitantly to the bride's father. The couple stepped forward together, the gowned minister blocking their view of the wooden cross.

The readings were short, the hymns unknown. The vows were made as instructed, and the rings were excitedly slipped on. It was all over very quickly. The couple, smiling politely, paraded back down the aisle to a fanfare of CD organ music which was slightly too loud. There were no photographs afterwards: they had all been taken in the hotel photo studio earlier that morning.

The family and friends were efficiently escorted from the hotel's 'Wedding Chapel' to a waiting room on the same fourteenth floor, where drinks were served. According to schedule, they were herded towards the reception room on the floor above. At a precisely choreographed moment, magnificent chandeliers dimmed and theatre spotlights homed in on the new couple as they entered through ornate double doors. Blinded, they steered their way past clapping relatives to the three-tiered cake. They cautiously took the 3-foot-long samurai sword and cut the cake.

A day like any other

This was a day like any other for the hotel. The schedule had been organized to the minute. The cake would be recycled, as the couple had only cut into a small piece of sponge cake inserted into the bottom tier. The delicious-looking, iced-in-plastic cardboard shell would be reused tomorrow.

A button pressed in the sound room brought another burst of music from the loudspeakers, as near-invisible hotel staff moved in to usher the bride out for a full costume change. They escorted her to a dressing room and wrapped her in full wedding kimono. A professional hairdresser styled her hair, and a make-up artist reinvented her face in traditional style. Twenty-five minutes later, they pushed her, breathless and unrecognizable, back into the reception hall to face more applause and more speeches.

The bride had not yet reached for her chopsticks, when the catering staff swarmed through again and skilfully delivered the next course, as unnoticed ushers spirited the bride and groom away for yet another costume change. They efficiently replaced the kimono with Spanish dress, and the groom changed into a colourful matador outfit chosen from the range offered by the hotel and hired by the hour. The pair re-entered to more applause, more food and more drink. I clapped along with everyone else.

The 'White Wedding', imported from a Western Christian heritage, is the most popular fashion for a marriage ceremony in Japan. Large hotels provide all-inclusive wedding packages: food, flowers, photos and formal wear, served with a full complement of professional advice, guaranteeing an elegantly designed ceremony and smoothly run reception, with a honeymoon suite available if desired. It makes for a fantastic occasion, at a fantastic price. The Japanese custom of guests donating gifts of money when they arrive at the hotel helps to offset this financial strain. There are wedding presents, but it is the guests rather than the couple who receive a gift as they leave. I struggle when I see couples married in such a 'Christian' atmosphere, in front of a cross, without Jesus being mentioned. But it is just for a day. It is just a ceremony. Ceremony is a highly valued aspect of Japanese culture.

For me living and working in Japan, ceremony is where I meet the public face of local culture. Adapting to the culture has meant much observation and listening, occasional questions, regular confusion and, I hope, humble learning. Wherever we live, we can be on the lookout for local expressions of culture. I grew up in Hull, and Sunday morning meant being down at the Boulevard, selling programmes for Hull FC. When I was living in Oxford, I led the May Day dawn parade down the high street with my accordion and a group of Morris dancers. Living in Northern Ireland in July provides an opportunity to see Protestant culture paraded through the streets. Public expressions of culture like these can be at turns enjoyable, intriguing, colourful and offensive, depending on where we stand in relation to them.

As we try to reach beyond ourselves, outside our own world and church culture into the lives of others, we will necessarily meet a different culture, maybe many different cultures. Each person we meet has their own culture, of which we must be sensitively aware as we approach them. Unfortunately, we often subconsciously see our own culture as superior, or consider our own way of doing things somehow better than others'. Try to ask questions about what other people do, without adding your own value judgment. Someone from Oxford recently asked me, 'I have quite a few friends who are from a Buddhist background. How should I relate to them? What should I know, what should I read?' These are the questions we need to begin to ask as we get to know people in our towns and cities who are from different ethnic groups, religious backgrounds, political affiliations, educational levels, social strata or generations.

Living together in peace

Shortly after their birth, Japanese children are taken by their parents to the local Shinto shrine. They return for special Children's Day ceremonies at the age of three and seven for boys, and five for girls. However far they move away, for university or work, they return home each New Year and visit the shrine with their family. While staying with the parents of a Japanese friend in my first ten days in Japan, I watched them prepare an offering of rice and sake (rice wine) to be placed in front of their Buddhist family altar each evening. I observed them bowing before it and praying. I have seen anxious students write prayers: 'Help me pass my high school entrance exams' or 'For entry into a prestigious university', and hang them at local Shinto shrines and Buddhist temples. I enjoy the splash of colour, as girls turning twenty don bright kimonos in mid-January and celebrate their coming-of-age ceremonies. I wonder over the use of pseudo-Christian wedding ceremonies. I don't always understand what is taking place on such occasions, but I watch and wait. I observe and learn. I try to understand beyond the barrier of culture.

These Shinto, 'Christian' and Buddhist ceremonies live together in harmony. My Japanese friends do not see any inconsistency here. They seem not to experience any clash of ideologies or conflict of religious values, and there is no sense of one religion stepping on another religion's toes. Rather, there is a genuinely sincere attempt to provide the most appropriate ceremony for each occasion. Whether children or adults or grandparents, there is a deep desire to make each occasion as special as possible. Maybe you have friends who would attend church at Christmas and Easter, use yoga to relax, and happily pray in shrines and temples in Thailand when on holiday.

When a young couple whom I had never met approached me as pastor of a church (in our case an elegantly designed white one with stained glass), to ask if I would marry them in church, I reacted inside with, 'How can you be so inconsistent?' But I have learned over the years that those inquiring simply wish to celebrate the occasion in the best available style. I have begun to realize that often ceremony is used as a way of alleviating the stress of uncertainty in any given situation. There is always a ritual available at each stage and event in life and death that helps, guides and comforts, many of which I still do not adequately understand. I have conducted many funerals in the UK, where the relatives were not clear, committed followers of Jesus, but still wanted a Christian service. When I do finally have some grasp of the origin and meaning of the ceremonies, I may not agree with them, but I must nevertheless accept that this is where my friend lives. As I get to know more people, I find that their understanding of their own culture also varies greatly. So even though I may think I have one area of Japanese culture figured out, I have to be careful to continue to listen and discern the other person's take on their own culture. If I were to ask people from Protestant families in Northern Ireland what their culture means to them, I would find many diverse answers.

This, though, can be said: everyone has had a lifetime of experience before I meet them, and most of that experience is foreign and inaccessible to me. So I have had to learn to stop, look and listen. I need to watch and observe. As I think and pray and love and wait, I remind myself that I know nothing about another person's uniqueness, except what they explain and show to me. And so much more of that needs to happen before anything I can blurt out about Jesus will be meaningful to them.

Engaging with culture

Jesus himself grew in his appreciation of, and engagement with, his own culture. Of the four Gospel writers, only Luke recorded a story from Jesus' childhood. Luke's purpose was to illustrate Jesus growing out of childhood into adulthood (in Jewish terms), while at the same time drawing our attention to Jesus' relationship with his heavenly Father, by portraying the tension with his earthly parents. We cannot therefore place undue weight on other details in the episode, but we do catch a glimpse of Jesus' engagement with the specifically Jewish religious culture of his day. I take it that Jesus accompanied his parents on most of the occasions Luke refers to: 'Every year his parents went to Jerusalem for the Feast of the Passover' (Luke 2:41). After many such visits to Jerusalem, when he was twelve (2:42), Jesus stayed behind there. Later his parents 'found him in the temple courts, sitting among the teachers, listening to them and asking them questions' (2:46).

We must be careful not to judge Jesus as precocious by our own standards. It was common in Jewish culture to sit together with rabbis. Asking questions was also standard rabbinic practice to generate useful discussion. Jesus was not teaching, merely entering into discussion and answering the rabbis' counter questions with surprising wisdom and understanding.

I visited Jerusalem while studying at Bible college. One day, a few fellow students and I were in among the crowds of tourists and pilgrims at the Western Wall. Black-robed Orthodox Jews were praying passionately at the wall and pushing prayer notes between the cracks in the stones. Tourists were congealing into photo groups, eager for fame in the plaza expanse. But my attention was drawn to a party, a riotous celebration, a dancing crowd of men, arms on shoulders, wearing resplendent colours and with voices joined in chorus. The thirteen-year-old boy at the centre of such passion was being transported, from childhood to adulthood. He held the scroll from the Torah and read with unrestrained pride. What privilege had come upon him, what growth and opportunity, what responsibility had been given to him now as a member of the adult Jewish community.

Jesus' visits to Jerusalem and his participation in rabbinic discussion were part of his growing up, his increasing understanding of himself and what it meant to be a Jew in first-century Palestine under Roman rule. At twelve going on thirteen, growing up in the country town of Nazareth, he may not yet have had much awareness of the political reality and all the devious machinations at a higher level of government in the vassal state of Israel. But as he moved into later teenage years and began working, he would begin to piece together such human knowledge. He accumulated it in bits and pieces from his parents and friends, from teachers and overheard conversations, from attending synagogue each Sabbath, and as he worked in the community with diverse groups of people, as he travelled to unknown areas with his parents. Like any teenager, he would have asked many questions and been dissatisfied with many of the adults' answers. I do not understand how the all-knowing Son of God was constrained to learn about Jewish first-century culture like this from the inside. Maybe it is partly why Japanese theologian Kosuke Koyama calls God the 'Three Mile an Hour God'. He walks with us at our pace. Jesus' largely unrecorded first thirty years of life were all about that, engaging with a particular culture from the inside by way of a single, unique, individual life.

Have a look around you

While living back in the UK one year, Alison was asked to help a Japanese woman living in Carrickfergus, Northern Ireland, to fill in some forms. The form required her to state her religion: Protestant, Catholic or 'other'. She was obviously going to be other, but what sort of other? Above the fireplace was a charm sent by her mother from her local Shinto shrine to ensure safe delivery of their second child. Alison hesitantly questioned, 'Is your religion Shinto?' Her easy response was 'No'. 'Buddhist?' Alison helpfully suggested. 'No,' she replied more confidently. 'No-one in our family has died yet.' It seemed an odd juxtaposition of cultural norms to be asking these questions in the UK. But such truly cross-cultural conversations are increasingly common.

Our own cultures are changing at a terrific rate. Rapid and highly varied cultural shifts in the UK, North America, Europe, Australia and New Zealand make it increasingly difficult to get a handle on the patterns of behaviour and mutual expectations of those with whom we share our high street. Globalization has brought swift, worldwide change to our previously homogenous localities. It is not only the public ceremonies like civil partnerships or non-religious funerals that mark a culture change. Moral attitudes shift in any culture by the decade. Our views of money and debt, sex and sport, are all subject to change. How we use words, how and to whom we show respect, how and what we are tolerant of, alter with cultural change. Even how we think, evaluate and make decisions about what is 'right' also undergo meta-morphosis. A Filipina Christian wrote, 'It is in the nature of culture to be invisible, presenting itself in recognizable form only in contrast with some other culture.'[2]

If we don't keep track of these changes for a few years, we can suddenly look into our own cultural backyard and not understand what we are seeing. The culture we thought we knew and owned has been insidiously supplanted by a new one, a foreign and alien one.

Pass the remote

How do we spot these incremental changes, some good, some bad, in our own cultures? When travelling to Japan, it was easy to adopt the role of learner, because I didn't have a clue what was going on. Learning to relate to people with understand-ing in such a finely structured and complex culture as Japan has taken – and continues to take – much time, effort, humility and courage. After any such four, tiring years, we return to the UK for a year, to be based in UK churches and UK culture (whatever it has become), where I have to unlearn many of my newly acquired Japanese responses and readjust to my home culture. So each time I return, I begin the laborious, but necessary, task of relearning my own changing culture. In the first few months, I take time to watch a lot of television. I have been told it is a good way to observe my own culture. Initially it is always a shock: the fashion styles have moved on, or back; jewellery is attached in a few more places than it used to be; I don't understand why the catchphrases are so catchy; I don't laugh at all the jokes – why are some of them funny at all? I haven't a clue who most of the celebrities are. When I watch soccer or cricket, athletics or the Olympics, I fail to recognize even the most well-known names. I am still embarrassed to recall that, returning one year before the World Cup, I had no idea who David Beckham was. So to find out what has happened to the culture, I have spent many unhappy hours flicking between channels, checking out that, just as I expected, things have changed. And how! However, having had to readapt to my own home culture four times in the last twenty years, I have found it a crucial process in limiting my mistakes and faux pas and learning to relate more sympathetically to others.

What do you watch on television? If you watch little, even for good reasons, choose a programme you wouldn't usually select and view it as if you are sitting with people who like to watch it. Enter their cultural world. Soap operas are a good place to start. They offer a condensed, intense version of a particular subculture, so try one set in your own country. You may not need to choose to watch television as consciously as I do. But as you watch, take time to examine your own culture. You may find that you have grown so accustomed to it that you take it for granted. You may find yourself wishing to dismiss it harshly. Somehow, we need to stand between these two attitudes, pulled in both directions, and allow ourselves to listen further. This is the beginning of learning where our friends and not-yet-friends gladly live and taking small steps towards their world.

I often listen in on chat shows and discussion programmes, which provide an opportunity to plug back into contemporary issues. The range of subjects brought up for discussion and public debate has widened considerably. I could not imagine many of them being broadcast even five years ago: two women living together wanting to adopt a child; cheating on your partner; psychics guiding your life. Don't limit yourself to programmes aimed at your own educational level. Watch one or two with participants from a different social, ethnic or religious background.

Of all cultural changes, language – and attitudes expressed through language – changes particularly slowly. Such change is more difficult to spot when you live in the same culture all the time, but it's essential to be aware of it because the influence is all the more pervasive. Four years away seems a long enough period for these changes to be noticeable enough that on return I have to relearn my own native language to avoid offending people. Social issues are dealt with in neutral, amoral language. The title in the bottom corner of the television screen informs me that it would be better if I raised topics with phrases like, 'Cheating on your partner', rather than attempting any debate on 'Committing adultery'. If I thought that essential new vocabulary was only needed in Japan, I was wrong. For example, I have to learn to refer to same-sex partners with equal importance and respect as husbands and wives. Language is learned by listening. So I make a conscious decision to listen to how people refer to same-sex relationships or different ethnic groups. I admit to eavesdropping on conversations in checkout queues, at bus stops and on trains, to hear how people refer to their mounting debt or mounting weight. In a UK culture that seeks to be highly tolerant of a wide range of opinions and positions, people are paradoxically offended by my misuse of language, which they consider patronizing, arrogant or paternalistic.

Take your time

Observing your own culture in this manner requires the temporary suspension of long-held personal values, and it takes a while to adjust. The longer I spend observing 'my culture', the more I begin to see. Discussions on television, for example, are well staged. They are designed to entertain the viewer. The presenter and choice of studio audience ensure that the viewer is exposed to many opinions on the subject. The audience's comments are personal opinions: 'This is what I think', 'This works for me', or 'I wouldn't do it.' The inter-action becomes more personal and emotional as the show progresses. But this need not lead to a clear understanding of the issue or a unanimous conclusion. Indeed, it rarely does. Topics are chosen, presented, discussed and left open.

I take time to ponder what viewers are seeking as they watch these programmes. Looking beyond the heat of such discussions, it seems that the underlying question for national perusal on a broad and bizarre (my cultural bias here) range of topics is: 'How can we best manage these situations?' No-one seems to be inquiring, 'Should we avoid them?' People are looking for help; they are asking, 'How can I get through this particular crisis?' They are not attempting diagnosis along the lines of 'Tell me what is wrong here.' The shows are presented as mutual self-help sessions, with the focus on 'What should I do?/What would you do?' They no longer seek to ask, 'What is right?' (my bias yet again). There is discussion with moral advice given among equals. The best guidance on offer is: 'This is what happened to me, so think about the consequences before you do it.'

My home culture has moved on again, and it has not taken me with it. Each time I am subjected to the process, it is less shocking, but it always requires an output of time, effort and emotional energy. How can you prepare yourself for this cultural adventure? How can you pull back the deficit of knowledge to be aware of the intricacy of the culture or cultures around you? In the next chapter, we will move on to how we meet people and relate to them. But first, what can we do to help ourselves be more aware before we even step out of the door or pick up the phone?

I often visit my local library where I can find a range of six or seven newspapers. I spread them out on the table to show as much of each front page as possible. I scan the headlines: 'Minister says yes to . . . ' (road infrastructure); 'What has happened to her face?' (celebrity watching); 'It's business as usual at . . . ' (local jobs); 'It's a farce' (human rights inquiry); 'One in eight women work past seventy' (retirement age rising). There are local papers concentrating on village news, others providing regional Northern Irish news and national papers offering UK-wide news. They are aimed at readers of different political persuasions, educational level and social standing. I usually spot an article that immediately provokes a strong reaction. Most often, it is an area where my own opinions are clear and differ most from the intended reader-ship of the paper. So I stop, put my bias on one side and try to take a step towards those who would enjoy reading the article. Why don't you visit a large bookshop and browse the best-sellers' section? Not because you like them, but to find out what other people are reading. If you want an extra challenge, buy one you wouldn't normally consider reading, not to bolster your arguments against it, but to understand more fully the world in which the readers of the book live. The internet is too large to consider any comprehensive interaction, so limit yourself to local sites: find out about the people, issues and attitudes of those living near you. As I do these sorts of things, I recalibrate my own cultural ears in regard to what people talk about and how they talk about it.

Have another look (at me)

There is a natural corollary to me taking a fresh view of my own culture, by which I mean the people who live near me, talk to me and relate to me as colleagues, friends and strangers: they also take a fresh look at me. This may be the most difficult change to notice and the most painful to accept, but it is imperative that we make an effort here before we open our mouths to talk about Jesus.

Let me illustrate this by describing how a Japanese person may see me. This is often how Western businessmen unversed in Japanese culture appear to Japanese businessmen. He is egotistic and rude. He is arrogant and conceited. He easily angers others and cannot apologize graciously. He is overeager to express his own puffed-up opinions. He forces himself forward and intimidates people. He is far from submissive or meek. He is spontaneous to the point of being rash. He does not take sufficient time to deliberate or consider others' advice before making a decision. He seriously disturbs the harmony of a group.

No-one would actually say that to my face. The culture doesn't allow it, but that is quite possibly what people think about me. This is all before I even mention that I am a Christian and a missionary, or that I believe in the Bible. If I do not learn to hear these silent voices and adapt to them, I condemn myself to exceedingly tough relationship-building and, on a human level, render myself largely ineffective in telling others about Jesus, or allowing God to reach out to others through me. In a new, unfamiliar culture that understands signals differently, that interprets body language more subtly, I need to be aware of how I appear through other people's eyes. This is ever more important in the UK today, because it has become a largely post-Christian culture, where respect for the church, for clergy, for Christians and the Bible has greatly diminished. I cannot change how others regard me at the outset of a relationship. But if I am aware of how they view me, maybe with disdain or suspicion, pity or hatred, I can try to find ways to adapt and minimize unnecessary hindrances.

When I first moved to Northern Ireland, I worked in a church, visiting sick and elderly members who were no longer able to attend church. They had never met me, so I greeted them warmly: 'Hello, Mrs Murphy. How are you?' The reply was often sharp: 'Where are you from in England?' My accent was a giveaway. The underlying message was: 'You are English and you don't understand our problems, so how can you care for me?' The culture barrier felt huge in the first three or four months. With a little language practice, after about six months I would visit someone I had not met before, greet them and the reply would be: 'How long did you live across the water?' In other words, my accent was somehow closer to Northern Irish, but also England-tainted. I had made half a step in their direction, and conversation about pastoral-care matters became easier. That was in the early 1990s. Since then, much of the bias against regional accents has disappeared across the UK, but we still need to notice what may be a barrier to heart-to-heart communication, and seek to address it.

Take a look at yourself

As cultures change, how they view Christians and the church also changes. We may consider that our role in society as

Christians and as the church of Christ has not altered at all. Theologically, of course, this is true, but the role accorded us by others may well have changed. How are Christians and clergy portrayed in the media, in sitcoms, dramas and documentaries? If we do not recognize this and adapt our behaviour accordingly, we risk making our task of forming meaningful relationships ever more difficult.

In the UK, for example, and maybe in your culture too, Christians and the church are no longer accepted as automatic authorities on anything. In open, public discussion, no-one is called upon to provide 'the right answers', partly because it would not facilitate open discussion. Who would you choose anyway? There are no right answers. There is no longer an agreed religious system to which all would submit to provide such a universal standard, and no accepted moral system that can bring objectivity to such a wide range of subjects. The cultural consensus has stripped 'right and wrong' of any intrinsic value; they are no longer regarded as acceptable ways of thinking. They are outmoded, extinct categories. The fashionable, acceptable modes of inquiry are: 'Is this for me?' 'Does it fit my lifestyle?' 'Will it work?' 'What will friends think?' These questions fire the process of decision and provide workable (just for me) answers. This comes as quite a shock if you are not used to it, and hard to live with if you believe the Bible to be true. But at least in this arena, I feel slightly more adaptable, having spent more than twenty years in Japan adjusting to precisely these dynamics. I remember in the early years thinking, 'If I am right (which I am, right?), why doesn't everyone listen to me and accept it?'

Such cultural relativity, whether historic in the case of Japan, or more modern as is the case for Europe, North America and Australasia, creates a particular problem for

Christians. Despite an 'anything goes – if it works for you, do it' way of thinking, despite a lack of absolutes, there is one issue on which everyone seems to agree. It is not stated openly, but nevertheless appears to be accepted as universal. It is: 'We will not tolerate those who think they alone are right.' We now live in a culture that is tolerant of everything except intolerance. People will listen to any opinion from any background, except someone who begins, 'This is right', 'This is true', 'You are wrong; I am right.' It is in such a context that I have learned to labour for Jesus and love others. So maybe I can be of some help to you where you are.

Maybe you have noticed that your own culture has changed slowly and imperceptibly around you. You may have occasionally remarked on it, but may not have actively attempted to identify the changes and adjust how you relate to people. The aisle of breakfast cereals has grown longer, and the payment methods (and not-yet-payment methods) are more numerous. The right to totally free, unquestioned personal choice, however, extends beyond the supermarket, twenty-four-hour shopping and online catalogues. It applies not only to consumer goods, fashion and alternative healthcare, but also to emotional needs, decision-making and personal identity crises.

Mind the gap

We have each grown up in our respective cultures, with our particular religious or non-religious backgrounds. We have developed a way of life unique to ourselves, influenced by our cultures, our personalities and our problems. Each of our lives is unique, by virtue of God's handmade act of creating us, and our own responsible (or irresponsible) acts have further moulded us.

When I meet someone, it is this double uniqueness, theirs and mine, that creates unfamiliar territory across which I have to navigate to be able to know the other person. They have a similarly tough task to cross the same territory to meet me.

4:

not what you know,
but who you know

Cut-throat conversation

I am lying back in the barber's chair, fish peering sideways
at me from their tank, as the five o'clock news summary
interrupts the sumo coverage. I have little enough hair to cut,
but the proprietors (in their late seventies) enjoy taking an
hour and fifteen minutes over it. I have had a scaldingly hot
wash and blow dry, and now I am lying back again having my
ears cleaned and shaved (yes, my ears). My forehead and even
the space between my eyebrows are treated to the cut-throat
blade.

As with hairdressers in any culture, we chat – about the
weather and the sumo tournament, about my two kids at
the local primary school, about their two grandchildren. We
touch on recent political events and sports. I mention a recent
wedding at our church. They have lived in the local area for
forty years, so they know of the Japanese family who began
the church. I have been having conversations with them like
these for eight or nine years.

After an hour and a quarter, I pay my £17 and step out into the sunshine, feeling the breeze on the back of my freshly shaved neck and the tingling of the lotions I always try to avoid having applied to my scalp.

Ten years ago when settling into a suburban area north of Belfast, I used a local barber's in the shopping centre. After a few visits, I let it slip that I worked for the church in Japan. The young woman cutting my hair excitedly announced to her friends in the shop, 'This man's a missionary.' I don't think she had met one before. At present I live in a rural area, and we shop in a village 3 miles away. It has a butcher-cum-baker's, a small supermarket and two hairdressing salons. So I enjoy the chance to chat with the hairdresser to gain a sense of the dynamics of small village life. The larger town near us has enough shops to make it easy to walk down the street unknown, ungreeted and largely ignored. But it does have a few coffee shops. I go regularly to the same one to meet friends or talk with other church leaders. The staff greet many of the customers by name. Friends chat with one another as they come in and out. A friend of mine who is a doctor took me to his local coffee shop. When ordering a second cup, the woman serving him asked for advice about her grandson who was ill. He didn't know how she had found out he was a doctor, but his explanation was: 'We come here most weeks.' After he had given the woman a few words of professional advice, he gently asked, 'What's your grandson's name? I'll pray for him.'

Things are not what they used to be

Making relationships used to be easy. When I was growing up in Hull, my best friend Jonny lived in the next street. My second best friend Andrew lived just across the road from me. We were in the same class at primary school. Though secondary school was a large twelve-form entry school, and I didn't share classes with Jonny or Andrew, we still played together after school most days.

At university I made many good friends, but they are now scattered all over the UK. We keep in touch loosely by email or irregular visits, but I have had few opportunities, living four out of five years in Japan. Our lives are no longer simple, family-based, local village affairs. For many legitimate reasons, changing jobs, marriage, housing or family needs, we soon find our relationships stretched – by a train journey, a car journey or a plane journey. Friendships are less easy to create and sustain. In our city-based lives, whether small-scale urban or megalomaniac metropolitan, cars, trains or planes allow us to live geographically separated from our workplace, church and friends. As Christians, we gather in church every week, drawn together by our relationship with Jesus and with one another. We travel quite a distance to do so. But a weekly church gathering will not help us form relationships with the 94% (or whatever percentage of your country is not yet Christian) of others. Rather, it is relationships at school and work, our recreational activities, hobbies and interests that provide us with natural opportunities to get to know others. In a word, it is life. Most of it is not organized or scheduled. It just happens where and when it happens.

Loving not your neighbour

For nine years we lived in a rented apartment block of twelve families, a ten-minute walk from the church. After a month or two, I began to recognize three or four of the mothers when they were standing outside, watching their children play on the path in front of the apartments. I didn't recognize anyone else who came and went. I never met the invisible husbands who lived with these wives. They left for work before I went out and returned well after I had gone to bed. They worked 'locally' in Tokyo, of course. I was unable to establish any relationships with men in our local area – apart from the barber.

In oppressive, urban Tokyo, with 30 million people within an hour or two's train journey, who do you choose to relate to? Who do you choose not to relate to? On what grounds do I make that decision? If I fancy Chinese noodles for lunch – I am told there are 21,000 Ramen shops (Chinese noodles) in Tokyo – which one should I try? The cheapest? The closest? The most advertised? One recommended by a friend? Where do you start?

Many of my friends in the UK live in semi-rural settings and work in the city. Their home is one of maybe a hundred that a developer built in a farmer's field. There is no shop, post office or petrol station. Both parents commute to work in different directions, and the children head off to school in yet another. There is no easy way to get to know the other people who live in the same field of houses, as they all live similarly busy-at-a-distance lives.

Some of my Christian friends live in villages a few miles from the city where they work. They ask me how they can reach out to the people in the village. My answer starts by encouraging them to truly live in the village. Have your hair cut there, use the post office every day, buy bread at the baker's, eat in the restaurant, sit in the park, and even go to the pub regularly.

I recently visited an open plot of land bordering three council housing estates. A pastor told me about the construction of the new church building that would begin next week. Unemployment is rumoured to be as high as 80% on one of the estates. But with no church members living on the estate, where and how should they start to reach out to the community? The pastor answered his own question later, as we chatted more over coffee. That week a woman had come into their present church building after the service had finished. She just wanted a cup of coffee. He had sat with her as she cradled the coffee in shaking hands and told him how her life was a mess, that she had to get out of the house, that she just needed a friend. She lives on that estate.

Planned and unplanned

As we read through the Gospel stories of Jesus' active years of ministry, we notice that he met and talked to people in many settings, and that much of his human interaction, especially with individuals, was unplanned and often even unsought.

Such seemingly random encounters happened more frequently when he was travelling, something Jesus did maybe more extensively than we imagine.

He walked south from Nazareth in the north-west to the Judean wilderness, east of the Jordan River, to be baptized by John. After returning north, he set up a centre of operations in the town of Capernaum, 20 miles north-east of Nazareth on the north-west side of Lake Galilee. From here, Jesus set out to visit a wide area. 'Jesus went throughout Galilee' (Matthew 4:23). 'Jesus went through all the towns and villages' (Matthew 9:35). In these places he sought opportunities to preach and teach. However, much of the material recorded by Matthew, Mark, Luke and John, in God's wisdom, happened in off-the-cuff, haphazard encounters with individuals.

After coming down from the Sermon on the Mount, Jesus met a leper (Matthew 8). A Roman centurion approached him for help in Capernaum (Matthew 8). Walking away from the house where he healed a paralytic, he passed by a tax booth and met Matthew (Matthew 9). When the crowds were pressing against him, a woman grabbed his cloak. On further-flung trips, he met people in a seemingly haphazard fashion, like the two demon-possessed men on the far eastern side of Lake Galilee. While in Tyre and Sidon, he met a mother with a demon-possessed daughter (Matthew 15). In Jericho, he bumped into blind Bartimaeus and spotted Zacchaeus up a tree. When visiting the village of Nain, he came across a funeral procession. (I don't imagine he had previously read about it in the obituaries column, prayed over it and decided to gatecrash the event for ministry reasons.) While simply walking away from the temple in Jerusalem, he was caught in conversation. Relaxing in Simon the leper's home in Bethany, he was anointed by a woman. On the way to his cross and death, he met Simon of Cyrene. Even in his last moments, he had a conversation with the criminal hanging beside him.

Most of these encounters were not organized or scheduled. They just happened. Jesus' first miracle doesn't look planned to me. He had decided to attend the wedding in Cana of his own accord: since he knew Nathanael from Cana, maybe he was responding to social expectations. But running out of wine was not something anyone had planned. That is why the wedding planning committee were desperate for help. Jesus happened to be there and responded, seemingly with a touch of reluctance.

As we read these stories, we like to jump straight to the action and skip the uninteresting links that describe the back-ground. 'While Jesus was in one of the towns . . . ' (Luke 5:12). 'As he went along . . . ' (John 9:1). 'It was winter, and Jesus was in the temple area walking in Solomon's Colonnade' (John 10:22–23). But if we linger a moment over the brief phrases that describe the settings for these encounters, we can see better how Jesus responded to people in live, unplanned situations. As Jesus walked in the cornfields, sat by the lake or climbed mountains, he related naturally to those around him.

Stepping out of your front door

As we step out of our front doors and walk along streets full of people we do not know, where and how do we begin to form relationships? I have had to unlearn a few things in Japan. I presumed I would begin by getting to know my neighbours, by which I mean those who live immediately on either side of our apartment. Some of you may live in communities where this is still the norm, expected social behaviour. If so, that is a great place to start. However, for the majority who live in urban areas, the people physically near us are often at a great distance relationally. My present neighbours would feel threatened and suspicious if I tried to develop a relationship with them just because I live next door.

I have asked hundreds of Japanese acquaintances what causes them the most stress and worry in their lives. The universal reply is human relationships. How do you relate to people older than you, younger than you, those you know well, those less so, in business situations or in neighbourhood associations? Japanese language and culture are largely concerned with this task.

Despite detailed and involved rules for interpersonal encounters, there remains the nagging doubt that, however hard you have tried, you didn't figure things out quite correctly and, in so doing, have unwittingly offended the other person. I have often considered the need for a theology of human relationships. I have wondered about sitting down with my Bible to see what I could come up with. It would certainly be good news for Japanese people. However, no human system, even based on the Bible, however ingenious, can fully describe or prescribe behaviour in an organic, living relationship. The dynamic of relationship cannot be determined beforehand, nor be considered once and forever fixed and dealt with afterwards. Relationship is fluid and susceptible to change; it varies in response to love and hate, pain and care, trust and betrayal.

As we saw earlier in the chapter, even in his earthly life Jesus did not provide us with a perfect, comprehensive, what-to-do-in-any-situation model of human behaviour. I believe he acted in perfect love and respect for those he related to in his human life, but he did not provide us with a foolproof method of relating to others. There is no method.

Those of us who grew up in close communities and now live in the city-scape of non-relating crowds of people need to recall this often and consciously adjust to it. Those of us who belong to churches that used to be the centre of small community life twenty or thirty years ago cannot presume any longer that those living in our community consider themselves to have any right of connection with our church, simply because they live next door. It used to be that a church bearing the name of the town or local area was regarded by people local to that area as 'their' church. That is rarely the case in urban situations in the twenty-first century. We need to consider a definition of locality, based not on distance, but on the more fluid and imprecise terms of human relationships. This will affect our concept of what it means to be a local church.

Who is my neighbour here?

Relationships begin with gentle listening, by being with someone in the hard times of sickness, grief, confusion and doubt. They involve sharing in the ordinary and simple things of life: shopping and cleaning, soccer and cars, books we've read and films we've seen. The church is full of ordinary people, with ordinary lives, who live simply alongside others. It is the ordinary people who have the crucial, indispensable role where church and community meet.

The opening question is not 'Can I preach the gospel?' or 'How can I get an opportunity to tell them about Jesus?' (we will come back to what to do about that in a later chapter), but initially it is 'How can I be a friend?' Or maybe even better, more humble: 'I need a friend.'

Often I find that both myself and many of my Christian friends are ill-equipped to take the best advantage of these encounters. We are too busy to invest our time in getting to know someone. We are too proud of our own priorities to give them up in order to relate to someone else. We are so caught up in our own affairs, making ends meet, making our dreams come true and organizing our self-made lives, that we do not have the time and emotional resources to give to others. We shy away from this simpler, longer-term way of living as salt and light that produces less immediate results. We may prefer to thrust a tract at someone rather than sacrifice our time, jettison our proud preconceptions and get to know someone who may live very differently from us.

Four or five Christian friends who live in a village in England with no evangelical church have an open-house pizza night twice a month. There is no formal content or structure to the evening: they eat and chat together. Recently, a couple of non-Christian friends accepted an invitation and joined them for the evening. The topics of conversation were quite random and not steered in a Christian direction. It was the first time the new couple had spent an evening in a room full of Christians!

Jesus was on his way back north to Galilee after a while in Jerusalem. He chose, against popular wisdom and culture, to walk back through the region of Samaria. Jews preferred to travel the longer way round and avoid the Samaritans, whom they despised as religious syncretists. We all know how Jesus befriended the woman at the well, went back to her village and stayed there a few days (see John 4:4–42). But none of this can possibly have been planned. Jewish men did not talk to women, especially Samaritan women, in an area they never travelled in. The village had probably never offered overnight hospitality to a Jew in living memory. Samaritan villages refused to provide such hospitality to Jewish travellers, in order to force them to travel the long way round. The religious animosity was mutual. Yet the most unthinkable and improbable thing happened, because Jesus was thirsty. And because this woman needed a friend.

People are desperate for friends – for friends they can trust. Surely, as followers of Jesus, we can bring a dynamic to friendship that is unique.

Not-so-local church?

As I mentioned earlier, defining 'local' by relationship rather than proximity affects our role as local churches and our approach to mission in our locality. In Tokyo, two competing dynamics, priority of relationship and separation by distance, have found a degree of resolution, resulting in a different concept of 'local'. The priority of relationship is seen, for example, in the fact that the Japanese much prefer to have a recommendation by a friend before approaching any new group of people, be that the doctor's or dentist's surgery, the kindergarten or tennis club or church. More often than not, a friend accompanies you and introduces you to a place. This also helps when we face the paralysis of too much choice and provides a human element of trust that allays the anxiety of not knowing where to go – something we will discuss in the next chapter. The second dynamic, separation by physical distance, is most clearly seen in an average, one-way daily commute of ninety minutes in the Greater Tokyo area. My own children, aged fourteen and twelve, having attended the local Japanese primary school a fifteen-minute walk away, adjusted to a forty-five-minute door-to-door journey to International School in Tokyo on a 7.30 rush-hour train each morning. It is this efficient transport infra-structure that allows the pull of human rela-tionship to overcome the physical separation by distance, and this results in an urban definition of 'local' as any-where within a sixty- to ninety-minute train journey. Thus, proximity is not measured in terms of linear distance, but in terms of ease of travel.

One of our church staff workers was employed as a businesswoman in the Ginza. She still travels an hour and fifteen minutes by train to see her doctor there. The Japanese pastor who has worked with me since graduating from Bible college, and has since taken over the church from me, would often drive his friends thirty minutes to his favourite coffee shop. Half an hour by car in Tokyo may be only a few miles (you could probably arrive just as quickly by bicycle), but you pass plenty of other coffee shops on the way.

Our practice of mission in the UK and similar cultures has been based historically around a parish understanding of 'local'. You research an area to survey the population distri-bution, note how large an area does not have a church, draw neat blue lines around it and claim it as 'unchurched'. You then buy or rent a building somewhere near the centre of this area and begin meetings. This is well suited to small rural settings, but not to large towns with a mass transport system or urban road planning.

If we look at a church in Oxford, Belfast, Sheffield or London, we will see how people increasingly move out of the local (I can walk there) area and travel/commute to church thirty minutes by car or train. It seems that we know fewer and fewer people in our immediate physically local area, because we commute to work and church and shopping and recreation. This is true not only of ourselves, but also of most other people. This must affect how we go about local mission and local church.

Large, growing churches in Tokyo, indeed in any of the world's larger cities, exploit the dynamics of the transport infra-structure, which in Tokyo means train lines (of which there are a bewildering number). The church where I worked for ten years sits conveniently between two parallel train lines, running out of Tokyo proper and east into the commuter belt as far as Narita International Airport an hour away. Most of the 150 people who attend Sunday worship services live within a few minutes of a station on one of those lines, and some may live equally close to the expressway that shadows it. Although 10% may walk, 15% come by bicycle, maybe 20% by car, and well over half travel in by train. Any friends they eventually introduce to the church are unlikely to live within a few minutes' walk of the building. If you invest a little time in plotting how long each member of your church travels on a Sunday morning and from which direction, you will begin to see in real physical terms what 'local' means in your particular church context.

So who and how?

In this flexible, even amorphous, setting, we need to know not only how to tell others about Jesus, but just as importantly who to tell. These two questions arrive together. They are interdependent. If I consider my task to be one of informing as many as possible in Tokyo of the basic gospel facts, I may incline towards mass-marketing and media opportunities to spread the information-message far and wide to the 30–40 million around the metropolitan area. If I consider that my task is to tell each of the people who live within half a mile of me about Jesus, then I would probably hand out tracts, visit each house in person or hold some meeting of interest for those close by. I am sure both approaches are used by churches near where you live, as they are in Tokyo. But just as human relationships are the key dynamic in Japanese social life, so they provide for us the most fruitful opportunities to introduce others to Jesus. This changes how we should approach local mission.

5:

who can you trust these days?

We can all remember our parents telling us, 'Don't talk to strangers, and don't take a lift from someone you don't know.' That was when, as children, we all walked safely to school each day and played in local parks on our own, even at a very young age. Few would feel safe enough to do that in many of our cities these days.

I passed through Shinjuku Station (central Tokyo) thirty minutes before the sarin gas attacks in 1995. A religious cult delivered a deadly nerve gas to five places on the rail system, causing twelve deaths, fifty permanent injuries and over a thousand cases of eye disorder. As a result, there was a tightening of the religious registration procedure and sharper vigilance over the activities of registered religious groups. But more damagingly, there was a strong sentiment among many Japanese that such small religious groups – Mormons, Jehovah's Witnesses, other religious cults, as well as the Christian church – could not be trusted. It suddenly became more difficult to encourage young children to come to church events.

A similar breakdown of trust has occurred in the minds and hearts of many in the UK who think the church can no longer be trusted, and so Christians cannot be trusted. It is hard for us to get used to living in this new situation, and we need some help to get our heads round the ramifications as we seek to tell others about Jesus.

'Nice weather today'

When we first moved to the Tokyo Metropolitan Area, we rented a fourth-floor apartment, ten minutes' walk from the well-established and growing Japanese church to which we had been assigned for training. Each day as I walked to the church, I tried to be inconspicuous, which is not so easy when you have brown hair, green eyes and your skin is a different colour. I walked with my shoulders sagging and my head down. I bowed my head tentatively whenever I passed anyone on the street. If I were to walk chin up, chest out, it would reek of arrogance; any cheerful 'Good morning' would be considered threatening by a casual passer-by. I knew everyone would be watching me to see whether or not I was a typical blustering foreigner. So I tried to fade gently into the background.

One woman living along the top road behind our apartment began to nod her head cautiously in greeting as I passed. After several weeks of this, the mutual acknowledgment became 'Hello' or 'Good afternoon'. Once or twice, she politely inquired, 'Are you an English teacher?' 'Where are you from?' I would stop and pass a few moments with her, replying minimally and without turning the conversation on her and asking any personal questions that could be considered threatening and invasive. Our conversations plateaued at the level of 'Nice weather' or 'Hot, isn't it?' My Britishness may have helped me to talk about the weather!

Then a few months later, she disappeared from sight. No matter what time of day it was when I passed the house, she wasn't out sweeping the road or tending to her flower boxes. I did not see her again for maybe a year, by which time we were due to return to the UK. She was outdoors again, but now her hair was grey, her face drawn, her posture fragile and her demeanour troubled. What had happened to her? The week we moved out, I called round to her house and rang the bell. I had bought her a small paperback book written by a well-known Japanese Christian author, Ayako Miura. I simply thanked her for her friendship, explained that I had missed her over the last year when she had not been around and gave her the book, with a deeper bow than usual. I passed on my concern for her to a church member who lived nearby and left it at that.

Four or five years later, word came back to me that she had been visited by that church member, had begun attending the church, had progressed to baptism and was now leading a local small group. My task had only been to gently establish an initial level of trust, and the beginnings of a relationship.

Come closer

There is a double wonder in Jesus' coming to us. He demonstrated that God is not distant. Jesus, referred to by John as 'the Word', 'was with God' (John 1:1). The preposition 'with' (in Greek, *pros*) also carries the connotation of 'towards', as in 'moving towards' or 'facing towards'. Jesus was eternally with God, facing towards God the Father in infinitely deep relationship.

In Matthew's Gospel, verbs of motion are used to signify attitudes of faith or of rejection of Jesus. This is particularly true of such verbs with the prefix *pros*. So the disciples were not merely moving towards Jesus physically (they 'came to him'), but more particularly they were coming to him with open hearts of love and faith.[3]

The first wonder is that, although Jesus was 'with' the Father and the Holy Spirit, he came into our world, 'and made his dwelling among us' (John 1:14). Jesus, God himself, made himself accessible to us. Looking back on the three years he had spent with Jesus during his earth-walking ministry, John summed up this wonder which he wanted to pass on to others: 'That which was from the beginning, which we have heard, which we have seen with our eyes, which we have looked at and our hands have touched – this we proclaim concerning the Word of life' (1 John 1:1).

The second wonder is the manner of Jesus' coming. John often uses the preposition *pros* to describe people moving towards Jesus. He wrote how John the Baptist 'saw Jesus coming towards him' (John 1:29). But it was the humble manner of his coming that made Jesus so approachable. Although he had no sin to confess, Jesus submitted himself to being baptized by John the Baptist. Much later, you may remember, Jesus 'came to Simon Peter' to wash his feet with the humility of a servant boy (John 13:6).

Andrew, having met Jesus himself, brought his brother Simon Peter to Jesus (John 1:42). Nathanael came to Jesus (John 1:47). More surprisingly, a Pharisee, Nicodemus, 'came to Jesus' (John 3:2) – even though it was night-time, and even though Nicodemus was a member of a religious group which would stridently oppose Jesus.

As we saw in the previous chapter, the Samaritan woman found Jesus accessible and approachable, despite the cultural, social and religious propriety that would have kept any Jew but Jesus from talking to this woman, and even from entering Samaria. The woman spoke to her fellow villagers, and 'They came out of the town and made their way towards him' (John 4:30).

A day or two later, Jesus returned to Cana in Galilee. A royal official, a man who worked for Herod, heard that Jesus was in Cana and 'went to him' from Capernaum and 'begged him to come and heal his son, who was close to death' (John 4:47). Great crowds of people came to him (John 6:5), and Jesus welcomed them, saying, 'Whoever comes to [*pros*] me I will never drive away' (John 6:37). Jesus was accessible, out and about with people: 'At dawn he appeared again in the temple courts, where all the people gathered round him' (John 8:2).

Of course, such approachability did not mean that everyone automatically came to him. Jesus spoke openly of those who 'refuse to come to me to have life' (John 5:40).

How accessible are our churches? Most church buildings remain locked during the week, and many have grilles or bars at the windows. Although such necessary precautions keep away unwanted burglars and vandals, they also make the building less approachable. Even if someone knocked on the door, would there be anyone to answer? I notice that, to offset this, an increasing number of churches are setting up cafés and coffee shops on church premises, in order to encourage local people at least to come in through the doorway. Many are allowing other non-church events to be hosted in their halls.

How accessible are our lives? With the increasing pace of life, we rush from one appointment to the next, and can be so driven by our schedules that we can easily give the impression that we have no time for those we come across during our day. We need to learn how to stand still for a moment, to stop doing the next thing on our personal agenda, and be quietly present to others. Maybe have a cup of coffee with someone, for no reason at all.

One year, a team from the UK led the children's programme for a week at our church in Tokyo. One quiet member, well over 6 feet tall, who must have seemed impossibly tall to the small Japanese primary school kids, simply let the children climb all over him during breaks and play times. They did not share a common language, but he made himself accessible and approachable. It reminded me of Jesus saying, 'Let the little children come to me' (Matthew 19:14).

My wife's home church is on the main road in what used to be a village that is now part of suburban Belfast. Urbanization, and particularly large supermarkets and car use, have largely destroyed the community lifestyle. Yet the church opens its two large halls once a week for a parent-and-toddler morning. Parents, guardians, childminders and grannies bring their kids, and often there are fifty or more, only one or two of them church familes. There is no formal content to the morning. But my wife and a few other church members chat with those who come. There is no pressure to make conversations lead anywhere. It is just about being accessible.

Fly me to the moon

The first time I travelled outside the UK, I was twenty-three. My increasing interest in Japan and my concern for the Japanese people led me to visit Japan and look for a job for a few years. Within two weeks of getting on the plane, I was staying in the students' dormitory of an English language school in Sendai, northern Japan, chasing two greasy fried eggs around my plastic plate with plastic chopsticks at breakfast. How do you get them anywhere near your mouth?

After a few weeks of strange breakfasts (rice, grilled fish, seaweed, omelettes, green salads and quite a few things I never managed to recognize before or after I ate them), I was presented with a two-page teacher's contract, which I duly signed. The first page stated the contract in terms of the minimum legal requirements for obtaining a visa. The second page supplied additional detail in conflict with those requirements. I didn't realize the significance of this until later.

A day or two later, we were at the Regional Immigration Office, sitting on black leather sofas around a low table and sipping green tea. The school's business manager, my potential boss, seemed to know the immigration inspector well. They chatted amiably for a while, although I had no idea what they were talking about. The documents were duly presented for my work visa. However, only the first page of my contract was presented. The second page of additional terms was not on the table. It looked as if everything was above board.

Who can you trust?

To me, a naïve Westerner, the school seemed to be openly flouting the legal requirements of immigration law in order to employ me. I couldn't accept it. 'This is a lie,' I said, in four poor Japanese syllables, pointing to the paper in the immigration inspector's hands. After a short conversation, the business manager ushered me out, embarrassed. The atmosphere in the car on the return journey was silent and cold.

Reflecting on this from a wise distance of over twenty years, I can see that the school business manager was asking me to trust him. I wanted to work for the school; he wanted me to work at the school; he knew how to get me a visa. All I had to do was trust him. There was one contract between the school and me, and another between the school and the Immigration Office. The immigration officer was probably aware that something was being held back. Japanese business is often carried out on multiple levels simultaneously. The forms are scrupulously adhered to, while much is left carefully unsaid, or vaguely hinted at and understood by the other party, without the embarrassing need to spell out the less acceptable details. Such silence in the conversation is heard and interpreted by other Japanese. The inspector's own silence may well have been a tacit response to the unspoken communication. How could I have begun to understand the intricacies and nuances of Japanese business dealings?

I naïvely thought that being right (and my understanding of what was right) was more important than trusting the business manager who wanted to employ me. I wasn't hired. Trust was irretrievably broken, and I was turned out of the students' dorm, with no money and nowhere to live.

Instant disciples: just add water

In chapter 1, we looked briefly at Jesus choosing his first disciples. Have you ever wondered how quickly Jesus chose those first disciples? Only the key defining moments of decision are recorded, not the whole process. Jesus had lived in Roman-occupied northern Palestine for thirty years before he picked them out and lined them up for the job. We sometimes jump from the Christmas narratives straight to the calling of the first disciples, without mentally passing through the intervening decades. A surface reading of the passages relating the calling of the first disciples may prompt us to think that Jesus was aimlessly wandering along the shore of Lake Galilee one day with nothing to do, and suddenly thought a few uneducated fishermen would be handy for boat-pulpits and general transport matters – not to mention walking-on-the-water training.

We can read six of the twelve disciples' stories. Andrew was a disciple of John the Baptist, who pointed him to Jesus (John 1:35–42). Andrew then introduced his brother Simon (Peter) to Jesus. Many think John may have been the other unnamed fellow disciple of John the Baptist,[4] who then introduced his brother James to Jesus. The two sets of brothers were partners and fellow fishermen on Lake Galilee (Luke 5:10), so they already knew and trusted one another. Philip met Jesus and introduced Nathanael to him (John 1:45). Philip, Andrew and Peter were from the same home town of Bethsaida, and it's pretty safe to assume that they knew one another. In fact, it shouldn't surprise us that half of the twelve disciples knew one another. Where trust is already established, it is so much easier to introduce others to Jesus.

On another occasion, Jesus asked if he could use Peter and Andrew's boat as a pulpit from which to teach the growing crowds. That day the brothers were feeling the weariness and frustration of having worked all night without reward, but they trusted Jesus enough at this point in their relationship to do as he asked. The unbelievable catch of fish and Peter's shock, 'Go away from me, Lord; I am a sinful man!' (Luke 5:8), shows how the relationship was continuing to deepen.

I don't think Jesus had had a predetermined list of twelve names beamed down to him from heaven directly after his baptism. I believe he travelled around his local area, before and after his baptism, having conversations and getting to know the people, the places and the wider boundaries of his own culture. Just as any initial warming-up of relationships takes place in countless insignificant steps over many chance encounters, and often without knowing ahead of time what fruit they will bear, Jesus had encountered many people during the early months of his ministry. He had got to know them in varying degrees. Then he went up a mountainside and spent the night in prayer. 'When morning came, he called his disciples to him and chose twelve of them' (Luke 6:13). I believe Jesus chose and called these men for his own reasons, in counsel with his Father, to fulfil his own purposes, and he took the divine initiative in each case. But those important choices were made within the context, and through the human process, of mutual, growing personal relationships.

Two of the three individuals God used to introduce me to Jesus were people I already knew and trusted. One was my best friend's father, whom I had known all my life; another was a school friend I had known for two or three years. The third was someone with whom I only shared a common Yorkshire accent, but even that somehow made her approachable. How about you? Who was most significant in your coming to meet Jesus? How well did you already know and trust them?

As my wife Alison and other church members chat to the mums at parents-and-toddlers about the weather, kids' colds, the struggles of bringing up children and other unthreatening areas of everyday life, without bringing Jesus into the conversation, people begin to talk to them more openly. Recently one woman responded to an invitation to study the Bible after two years of gentle conversation. So now, she and a couple of church members meet on another morning, where that trust is deepening.

Taking your time

In Japan, business relationships are bound together with trust, established over many years. This trust is not won by exchanging all available information on the first day. Japanese companies wine and dine prospective clients a number of times before agreeing to do business together. Details are worked out afterwards, because they trust one another to find workable resolutions to any problems. Many Western businessmen try haggling over contract details while drinking the first cup of coffee. Such an atmosphere is quickly perceived by Japanese as distrust and precludes doing further business together. The non-Japanese businessman may never spot what went wrong. From his point of view, he may even believe that he had gone about business impeccably. But without trust, there is no relational base from which to move into further business dealings.

In Japanese society, trust is not easily or quickly won, and when lost it is almost impossible to re-establish. Distrust is an invisible barrier that is difficult to penetrate. A Japanese specialist in social withdrawal syndrome (*hikikomori*), a uniquely Japanese affliction where people shut themselves off from social interaction, explains that the Japanese begin with a distrust of people: 'Distrust is so rampant that spouses can't be transparent with their spouses, nor parents with children'; 'A child's core belief is "I cannot trust my parents, and therefore others."'[5] Any human relationship, particularly a new one, is viewed with suspicion and has to be entered into with extreme care. Opinions are not expressed openly in the early stages of a relationship, since the speaker does not know how they will be received. There is a lot of careful mutual manoeuvring before any degree of trust can be established. This is, of course, an even more involved process where religion is concerned, and is compounded further in the case of Christianity, which is considered exclusive and foreign. In Japan, trust is the product of many years of careful observation and small-scale interaction over an extended period of time. It is established with great care, but once in place is enduring and loyal.

Breakdown

How does an understanding of these dynamics help us to be better prepared to pass on the unique truth of Jesus to those living in our own towns and cities? Twenty years ago it probably wasn't necessary. The Christian church in the UK, for example, had been trusted and respected for centuries. Biblical values were upheld as cultural norms, and Christian lifestyles were considered trustworthy. Church leaders and members had trustworthiness conferred on them by association. They didn't have to work that hard to be trusted by others. In the UK, at least, that is no longer how people feel towards the church or towards Christian believers.

This change has occurred for many reasons, with its origins both within and outside the church. For example, a liberal approach to Bible interpretation cast doubt on the trustworthiness of the Bible text. Church leaders involved in financial or sexual scandal brought leadership into disrepute. Many people have been wounded by the overzealous strictures of their own religious upbringing. Legalism, moralism and hypocrisy in the church have damaged the public understanding of the Christian worldview to a point where it has been demoted to a position of redundancy or irrelevance for the average person. A siege mentality in the church has often twisted well-meaning love-your-neighbour outreach into a convert-grabbing caricature from which our neighbours have learned to run away. Our tolerant, multi-ethnic society objects to our audacious claims about the uniqueness of Jesus. People are suspicious of our intent when we approach them to talk about Jesus or to invite them to a church meeting. That suspicion grows into open contempt when we claim we speak with spiritual authority or say Jesus is the only way to God, without having first established a degree of trust.

Can we fix it? Yes, we can

Re-establishing trust after it has been broken is a long, involved and arduous task. A generation ago, when many people were in sympathy with the position and goals of the church in society and the church was a familiar place, mission was largely concerned with encouraging people to heartfelt repentance and warm acceptance of Jesus as Saviour. It was thought to be a relatively quick process, achieved by well-meaning, sincere urging. Even in my student days in the early 1980s, this was still a common approach.

But for many people, church is now an old-fashioned, irrelevant or unacceptably arrogant and hypocritical institution. For those who are antagonistic to church as an establishment and critical of Christian ethics and lifestyle, our approach to mission needs to be radically reassessed. Just as in Japan, we must first seek to re-establish trust, to make an effort to rebuild credibility. We must approach others with humility and live out our faith in Jesus with a gentleness and patience that draws others into approaching us. For the tens of thousands who have been hurt by religious institutional life or put off by their own church experience, this will be a long, loving task. For the thousands in different faith communities, it will require patient, persevering, humble attention.

In the present cultural climate, our claim to speak the truth, to represent Jesus who is the Truth, is an immediate barrier to friendship and an initial obstacle to trust. And to press on with our preaching in an even louder voice is to add bricks to the wall of distrust. Without trust, our words of truth will have no medium through which to travel to reach the hearts of those wandering in their own darkness, and our claims regarding Jesus will be considered spurious and suspicious. No-one will be willing to listen to us, however true our message is. We need to remove bricks from the wall of distrust, and this brick-by-brick process may take a while.

caring for others

Love is . . .

'Now we know what love is,' said a Japanese student on return from three weeks' homestay with a Christian family in the States. The remark brought nods and similar comments from most of the twenty or so who had been on the Homestay Program to Ohio (including this British man, who had helped to prepare them for the trip and travelled with them, even though he had never been to the US before!). The families had saved for eleven months of the year in order to be able to host a student. They provided homely hospitality and took the student out sightseeing a few times. But most importantly, they simply welcomed them into their family for a while. Many Japanese in their twenties and thirties have been deeply touched by the love and care shown to them by Christian families while abroad for a year or more in the USA, Canada, UK, Germany, the Philippines, Singapore, Australia and New Zealand. The love and tenderness with which Christian families invite them into their homes and family lives breaks down barriers of mistrust or suspicion and very often leads the students to begin thinking about Christianity, or attending a church when they return to Japan.

A quarter of the Chapel of Adoration congregation have lived abroad for a year or more, all with positive experiences of Christians looking out for them.

Jesus told the story of a Samaritan man who helped a Jewish person. The devout Jews of Jesus' day despised this racial group for their mixed religious beliefs, and avoided any social contact with them (see Luke 10:30–37). The telling point of the story is that the Samaritan man went out of his way to cross the barriers of class, race and prejudice to help another.

With increasing globalization, even in small towns, there are people living far from their home cultures whom we can befriend. Many come from cultures that are more open to chatty conversation and would readily respond to caring questions: Where are you from? How long have you been here? How are you finding life in the UK? With the growth of the church in many places in Africa and Latin America and some parts of Asia, you may even find people who have a positive view of the church. Don't be surprised if quite a few are Christians.

Showing people that we care for them is a crucial part of bringing people along in their journey to trust Jesus.

Needing help

One day, a church member was sweeping in front of the church on the main road, when a balding, brown-faced man approached her and asked, 'Is this a church?' Mr Sato lived 500 miles away, but his daughter lived in Ichikawa (where the Chapel is). She had collapsed under the strain of work and been admitted to a psychiatric hospital for treatment. Her mother was not well enough to travel up from Osaka, so her father had come to stay in his daughter's apartment to visit her every day. He didn't know anyone in the Tokyo area or where to turn for help. He was suffering sleepless nights and was beginning to worry about his own mental health. Although he knew nothing about church, his interest in literature had left him with the impression that the church was the place to go for help. So that day, feeling that he could no longer carry on all alone, he had begun walking the streets of Ichikawa to look for a church.

Sitting in our bright, café-like downstairs room, Sozo (our assistant pastor at the time) explained how a Japanese family had built the church, how they had had a famous car-racing son, Tojiro. 'Oh, I knew Tojiro,' Mr Sato interrupted brightly. Recalling events forty years earlier, he said, 'The day he crashed I was at the race circuit. I went to the hospital with him. When I saw them remove the steering wheel from his car, I knew he had not survived.'

In his loneliness and desperate need for support, Mr Sato began to come to church every Sunday. He completed the beginners' Bible study we hold after the service. He came to the Wednesday night prayer meeting and met weekly with Sozo to study Exodus. He brought his daughter to church occasionally when she was feeling up to it. He soon reached a decision that he wanted to become a Christian. Within a year or so of his baptism, with his daughter discharged from hospital, they both returned to their home town, Osaka. Mr Sato now serves there as a deacon in a local church.

Why did this man, and another we will meet shortly, come to the church for help? In a country with far fewer than 1% who are Christian, why did they seek help from the church? Not because we gave out tracts: we do very little of that. He had not attended our concerts or had any previous contact with anyone in our church. Even in a country with so few Christians, these men had picked up that Christians care for people and that the church is a place to go for help. They turned up unknown and unannounced, the result of others bearing witness to Jesus as the Way. They were small plants about to burst into life from seeds that had been sown by other unknown individuals. They came as a consequence of Christian mission, but not as we might recognize it or practise it.

Disorganized miracles

We all know that Jesus performed many miracles in his brief years of public ministry. For example, at the end of Matthew 4, after the calling of the first disciples and before the pronouncement of the Beatitudes in chapter 5, there is a description of a typical occasion when Jesus was 'healing every disease and sickness among the people . . . people brought to him all who were ill with various diseases, those suffering severe pain, the demon-possessed, those having seizures, and the paralysed, and he healed them' (Matthew 4:23–24). Following along in Matthew's account for a while, we see the variety and diversity of Jesus' miracle-studded activity. The Sermon on the Mount is barely over when Jesus meets a leper who begs to be made clean. Jesus heals him, and then in quick succession he heals a Roman centurion's servant and Peter's mother-in-law. This all happens in the space of a few hours, and that evening it is followed by further healing and exorcisms. What connects an outcast leper, a hated soldier of the occupation and a mother-in-law? What thread connects leprosy, paralysis on the verge of death and a fever?

The scope of Jesus' activity quickly outgrows our capacity to categorize it. He calms the winds and waves of a storm on the lake and then casts out demons into a herd of pigs. He heals a paralytic, raises a dead girl and heals a chronically sick woman, the latter unconsciously. He barely pauses before he restores the sight of two blind men (Matthew 9). There is no plan or organization here. Why is Jesus' ministry so full of seemingly random encounters? A hint of an answer lies in Matthew 9:36: 'When he saw the crowds, he had compassion on them, because they were harassed and helpless, like sheep without a shepherd.' He was caring for those he met on the street, in the villages and even beyond the villages. Every act of kindness and care touches someone's heart. Every day we are surrounded by opportunities to be kind and caring: to carry a heavy shopping bag for an elderly woman; to help lift a buggy off a train for a young mother; to give directions to someone who looks lost; to sit quietly on a bench by someone who looks lonely and talk about the weather. What can you do today?

Desperate

Often we do not see the results of our acts of kindness. It was Sunday afternoon, and a man with grey hair, weathered skin and old clothes walked into the church grounds and approached me with, 'Would you have anything to eat?' I slipped back into the church lounge, where there was a meeting in progress, picked up one of the remaining lunch boxes and slipped out again. He accepted it with simple gratitude. I went back in and quickly made him a cup of tea, which he drank while he ate, sitting in a quiet corner of the grounds. Sometimes he comes on a weekday, so I walk with him to the convenience store and let him choose his own lunch. He knows he can come any time.

At other times we are part of the story long enough to see our kindness bear fruit. One man, in his sixties, was homeless when he came to ask for help. The family who started the church provided him with a place to stay for a few months. In time, he began to attend the church services. We introduced him to a local pastor who worked with homeless men, and he was given long-term accommodation. He has since been baptized and works alongside the pastor in his charitable organization, seeking to help other homeless people in the area. Every time I see his smiling face as he cycles around our area, I am glad for the little we were able to do for him.

ID card, please

God uses our willing kindness to people to soften their hearts. Sometimes it will be known that we are Christians, other times not. Jesus did not heal every sick person in Israel that week. He was restricted to one place and had a limited number of hours in his day. So, shortly after this, he called on his key twelve followers to spread this compassion-filled ministry (Matthew 10:1–8). The initial manifesto (these days it would be labelled as a church strategy or vision) was not focused solely on preaching, but included healing and exorcism. These were visible signs that showed that the accompanying words, 'The kingdom of heaven is near', were more than empty slogans. They were the announcement of a new reality.

This activity occurs in the early part of Matthew's account of the coming of the kingdom. It shows how Jesus gained the interest and attention of the common people. I would venture to suggest that the colossal impact Jesus made in these days was not only because of the supernatural origin of the acts themselves, but also due to the depth of his compassion: each and every miracle without exception was performed because he deeply cared about the person involved. His compassion transcended the boundaries of gender, social status, hatred, prejudice, religion and even faith. The only common theme in these miracles was that Jesus cared for the persons concerned. This, more than the mere display of raw power, had the capacity to generate the huge following and passionate (if fickle) response of the ordinary people.

Not all who witnessed Jesus' powerful kindness were attracted to him. Those who considered themselves to be a few privileged ranks above the merely 'ordinary' found such care-full activity deeply unsettling. When Jesus healed a man with a shrivelled hand (Matthew 12), he was castigated by the Pharisees for 'working' on the Sabbath. Jesus likened his active care to pulling a helpless donkey free from a pit. His point was that the Pharisees used the right words, but lacked compassion for people. We may be very familiar with Jesus' words: 'For they do not practise what they preach. They tie up heavy loads and put them on men's shoulders, but they themselves are not willing to lift a finger to move them' (Matthew 23:3–4), but we are unsettled if they are applied to us. In post-Christian UK, and similarly in other countries with long Christian histories, sadly many people have found the church's attitude to others hypocritical and have become cynical of the claims and relevance of Christianity. To such people it is only our ongoing and outgoing kindness that can prepare a way for future conversations about Jesus.

Do you know a lonely person who would like company over a cup of tea? Someone who shuts him- or herself in the house who you could offer to accompany on a short walk? Do you know anyone who is ill, whom you could help with the shopping? An elderly person to whom you could offer a lift? A single mother you could help by babysitting for an hour? Think of all the people you know, find someone who would benefit from a small act of kindness and start there. You may be surprised at what God does.

Caring for others

Jesus had compassion on people and healed their sick. He miraculously fed a crowd, including 5,000 men (Matthew 14), not just to prove who he was, but because he cared that they were hungry. At the time, Jesus was suffering shock and grief at the news of John the Baptist's cruel execution (Matthew 14:1–12). Andrew, who found the boy with the meagre lunch, must also have been hurting over his former master's death. Yet they continued to care for those around them. Jesus didn't walk on the water for the fun of it: he went to help the disciples because they were buffeted by the waves in a strong headwind (14:22–27). The 'lame, the blind, the crippled, the mute' all came to him because he cared for them: 'I have compassion for these people; they have already been with me for three days and have nothing to eat. I do not want to send them away hungry, or they may collapse on the way' (15:30, 32). This further miracle of feeding 4,000 people was a simple act, motivated by heartfelt compassion.

If Jesus didn't try to open people's hearts with words alone, neither should we. We must accompany – and precede – our words about Jesus with the same care that Jesus showed. He met thousands of people – some followed him; others did not. Some had faith in Jesus; others did not. But in every case, Jesus cared for them. Jesus' miracles certainly were extraordinary displays of power, but I suspect that those involved were more deeply moved by their experience of his personal, involved, unconditional, gracious loving care. Jesus spoke against the religious hypocrisy of his own day on many occasions. In Matthew's Gospel, it was the last issue Jesus taught on publicly before his arrest and subsequent crucifixion. He told the hard-hitting parable of the sheep and the goats (Matthew 25:31–46) to emphasize the urgent need to care for people. We dare not be content with well-meaning religious talk. We must combine it with authentic, caring action.

Do we care?

In the UK, as in many other countries, we face huge social problems. This is not new. It has always been so. In these early days of the twenty-first century, we face issues such as obesity, drunkenness, drug abuse, domestic violence, anti-social behaviour, mental illness, date rape, racism, religious hatred and homelessness, to cite just a few.

As Christians, we can and must care for those who have been victimized by such tragedies. How can we care for those in our communities who have lost a son to suicide, a daughter to rape, their house to loan sharks, their health to AIDS, their well-being to stress, their marriage to violence, their sanity to violent hatred? How well we care for the hurting and wounded around us establishes our credentials for carrying the message of hope – the gospel of Jesus – to such people.

In recent generations, the church in the UK has largely lost its reputation of being a place that cares for others, and is all too quickly forgotten as an irrelevance. We must regain that credibility, both in our individual lives, and also with practical, hard-working projects in corporate church life. I am not advocating a social gospel that tries only to help people and leaves it at that. As we will see, the verbal proclamation of the truths of the gospel is paramount. But without showing full-blooded care, we strip ourselves of any authentic base from which to pass on the unique message of hope that Jesus brings.

This does not mean that your church immediately has to start up ten separate groups – to help the homeless, teenage mothers, AIDS patients, rape victims, battered spouses, trauma casualties and drug addicts. What I suggest is that, in addition to showing kindness to those you know and meet on an individual basis, you also look around and find out what Christian-run projects there are in your town or city. Maybe there is an alcoholic rehabilitation centre, a rape crisis centre, drop-in facility for the homeless, single-parent hostel, debt management advice centre, ex-young-offender hostel. Learn about them, talk about them with friends, support them by occasionally helping out or giving. Publicize them in your church and local area. It doesn't matter if they are not run by a church like yours. If they are managed by a different denomination, you will double the benefit by working against the common perception that individual churches are partisan, separatist and interested only in themselves. If you look around your city, county or nearby larger cities, you may be surprised at what is going on.

Many around us are suffering. Richard Foster, in his book on prayer, comments that Christians are unique because we believe in suffering: ' . . . we stand with people in their sin and their sorrow. There can be no sterile, arm's-length purity. Their suffering is messy business, and we must be prepared to step smack into the middle of the mess.'[6]

Jesus' incarnation and passion show us the redemptive nature of joining others in their suffering. Each facility and Christian help centre says to others, I believe in being with you in your suffering. As you meet people, hear the local news, observe with Christ-like tenderness those who live on your street, you will find many opportunities to care for others. The degree to which we care for others is being scrutinized by all who have a negative view of Christianity. It is a gap that only loving care can begin to bridge.

The lonely, the hurt, the marginalized and the confused do not know where to go. The number who would consider seeking help from Christians, or from your church, will depend largely on their experience of other Christians, and of the church as a caring community. Welcoming them can be one of our biggest opportunities to display the uniqueness of Jesus to our world. We cannot help everybody; nor is the church the only caring establishment around. But if we care with the tenderness of Jesus, modelled on him, and lived out by the risen Lord who dwells in our hearts, we will be noticed and recognized as those who care. If you reread the early chapters of the Acts of the Apostles, you will see what that looked like in first-century Middle-Eastern culture. How would it look in the twenty-first-century culture where you live?

Don't worry if you don't feel you have it all together to help people. You don't have to provide answers to all their problems. Most people are looking for company and faithful support in their struggles, while they work out what to do. I didn't know, for example, how to solve Mr Tanaka's problems.

In trouble

He wanted to talk to me alone.

'My wife has walked out on me.' Mr Tanaka's business career was successful, but his marriage was not. He and his three-year-old boy moved back in with his parents, a ten-minute walk from the Chapel.

Despite his apologies and desperate pleas, his wife would not come back and live with him, so he had sought help from a church. I listened to his story and prayed with him that his wife would return, but when I met with him again a few weeks later, she had filed for divorce. At the court hearing, Mr Tanaka pleaded to be allowed to restart his marriage. During this period, he began to attend church regularly, and his son settled in Sunday school. Many people in prayer groups around the world prayed for him by name. However, his wife stubbornly pursued the divorce, which was granted. Surprisingly though, his wife did not pursue custody of her son.

After a few more months, Mr Tanaka came to baptism, expressing a deep conviction of his unworthiness, with his son kneeling beside the baptistry. Mr Tanaka's face was burnt brown by the sun, from hours spent reading the Bible outside. He decided to use his business skills to help with church finance, and planned the primary school Christmas event – in July! He even sold his luxurious car and called on me to bless his new Jeep, which he felt was more appropriate to his new lifestyle. He serves as church treasurer, handles much of the awkward but necessary legal paperwork, tax issues and registration requirements, and he has become a key member of the church leadership team.

And yet I did nothing more than support and accompany him on his journey and watch God at work in his life.

church: finding a way in

Escape route

Hanako, heartbroken after breaking up with her boyfriend, escaped to the UK for a few months to study English. On the way to the supermarket one morning, she dropped her shopping list. It was picked up and politely returned to her by another Japanese woman walking behind her, who, recognizing the list was in Japanese, began a conversation. She introduced Hanako to a Japanese couple working with Japanese in Cambridge. Hanako went round to their house for meals, for friendship and then for Bible study. When she decided to return to Tokyo, the couple encouraged her to attend a church and recommended the Chapel of Adoration. When Hanako came to the church, knowing no-one, she was surprised to find that the woman who had picked up her shopping list in Cambridge was in the congregation.

Hanako came to the church every week. Afraid of what her family would say if they knew she was going to church, she told them she was 'just going out' on Sundays. After the service, she would stay on for lunch. As our downstairs room filled up with people eating their rice-and-whatever lunch boxes, she would find a table with a few students or those in their early twenties and eat with them. Most Sunday afternoons the group would find a spare room and have a time of informal Bible study, prayer, sharing and singing together, with a mature Christian couple in their thirties on hand to give gentle, wise pastoral care where needed. The group would hang out together for a few hours. Some time after three o'clock, they would return their borrowed Bibles and song books and saunter back into the Chapel's café-like main downstairs room. There would usually be a few people hanging around: a group of kids outside skipping or throwing a ball and their parents who couldn't go home yet because their kids didn't want to leave. Others in twos and threes might be drinking tea, chatting or praying. If any of the younger folk wanted to linger longer, they could do so.

The longing for belonging

In the UK, as in many developed countries, our affluence and materialism provide a rich surplus of gadgets, but fail to nourish personal relationships and a sense of belonging. I am sure you can see signs of this wherever you live: young people leave home; parents, married or not, are working so hard that they have little time for each other or the needs of their kids; children are raised for a while, then passed around at service stations at weekends, as reminders of broken trust; older people leave marriages they have been in for decades; as grandparents grow older, they are cared for by paid staff. No-one has much spare time to give to any larger group that might demand their loyalty.

In an increasingly fragmented society, how and where can those from relationship-wary, trust-scarred backgrounds find security and belonging? How can we reach out to them, melt their fears with love and provide sanctuary for them while they find a way to Jesus?

We each have a deep-seated, human need to belong. However much our culture may have altered, the basic human need to be part of a community remains. The problem we face as a church, and as individual Christians, is that most people in the UK and maybe in your country too, when they ask themselves whether church is for them, give the following answers: 'No, it's not for me; I don't want to belong to that sort of group; they are not the type of people I want as my friends; I couldn't be open with Christians about my inner desires and struggles; they wouldn't listen; I don't think they will accept me; I don't think they will love me; they will judge me for who I am and what I have done.'

Our Christian communities, whether families, small groups or larger Sunday gatherings, need to be places that surprise these people. They should be environments that nurture trust toward Christians, the church and therefore Christ. We need to live together in authentic harmony. Loving one another as Jesus loves us is more easily done, and seen to be done, in smaller groups, with less rigid structures than worship services. Some of these groups will be weekday groups, some weekend groups, some after-church groups.

Holding hands in a circle

Do you remember Sachiko whom we met in chapter 2? Her story illustrates the long process of becoming a follower of Jesus, and maturing into a person who then leads others to Jesus. She was a young mother with a child at nursery school, when she was invited to attend one of the Ladies' Circle groups held in the church on Tuesdays, Thursdays and Fridays. We have a purpose-built living room – split-level, bright and spacious, with sofas and a television – in the church. Church members find meeting here less stressful than hosting a meeting in their own homes, which tend to be tiny and a long distance away. In many other countries, meeting in a person's home would be ideal.

Japanese pay great attention to what any group is called. Most possible titles convey an exclusive dynamic: members only. Like 'Presbyterian Women' or 'Baptist Ladies' or whatever your church's equivalent may be. The title 'Circle' was chosen because it has an inviting flavour, like a craft group – anyone is welcome. As Sachiko experienced, these groups of five to eight women welcome non-Christians, befriend them and walk alongside them as they find their way into this unfamiliar world and discover what it means to follow Jesus. The group provides support and care, as women find their way to an individual trust in Jesus.

The Japanese pastor with whom I was working after graduating from language school told me, 'Japanese become Christians backwards.' He meant that they come into the church, form relationships within a group of Christians and find their way to individual faith supported by the security of belonging to that group. At the time I strongly disagreed, and put forward my very Western theological arguments. However, continued observation has proved me wrong. In a group society like Japan, this is what happens. I have seen it in each of our small groups. I have since also noticed it in the UK: non-Christians may join a parent-and-toddler group in the church, then begin a Bible study, Alpha or Christianity Explored course, and over many months, or even years, of support and care, they commit themselves to following Jesus.

Japanese interpersonal relationships have followed the pattern of Confucian ethics for many centuries, emphasizing a duty of obligation to one's elders and responsibility for those who are younger. Human interpersonal relationships are complex and emotionally demanding. Consequently, any new relationship is begun after lengthy consideration. Japanese will watch and observe someone for a long time before beginning, gently and cautiously, to relate to them. This process is even more involved when joining a religious group, because the ensuing relationship comes with an extra set of expectations and values.

Thus, when a Japanese person first meets a Christian, then maybe attends a small group or church service, he or she will engage in the process of counting the cost of belonging to the group. Of course, in the initial stage there is a huge information gap: they have never been to church before, never held a Bible before, never celebrated Christmas or heard of Easter. It takes a while to cover the basic ground of the Bible's story of God and humankind.

But at the same time, the Japanese are conscious of the emotional process of exploring the dynamics of the human relationships within the group. They are not used to meeting people who are open about their struggles, who make themselves vulnerable and weak. Their first impression is probably to ask, 'Is this for real?' In a culture where human relationships are highly choreographed and manners are professionally manicured, they will find the unburdened joy of relationships and the unpretentious openness of Christians both unexpected and attractive. Non-Christians are evaluating the authenticity of the discipleship they see in us, rather than the orthodoxy of the preaching. They are assessing the reality of our relationships with one another and with Jesus. I find that challenging and scary.

In most postmodern, post-Christian countries – UK and Ireland, USA and Canada, Australia and New Zealand and mainland Europe – Christians are often viewed with suspicion or disdain. The authenticity of our discipleship, how we follow Jesus, is under scrupulous observation. Superiority, hypocrisy or any sniff of elitism on our part will seriously put people off.

Do I or don't I?

People gathered in groups around Jesus. They observed, listened and inquired about deeper commitment to his amazing teaching. As we have seen in previous chapters, Jesus taught on hills, in boats and in homes. His teaching was intriguing and attractive. After a while, some of those listening began to approach him with deeper issues, with personal questions about following him.

For example, one man asked, 'Teacher, what good thing must I do to get eternal life?' (Matthew 19:16). Jesus replied, honestly spelling out the true cost of being a disciple, 'Go, sell your possessions and give to the poor' (19:21). For this man, it seems, the cost proved too great: 'When the young man heard this, he went away sad' (19:22). The disciples had been watching the encounter, maybe expecting that the rich would be welcomed more eagerly into kingdom life. They took up the theme of the conversation and, probing further, let Jesus know that they also had considered the cost: 'We have left everything to follow you!' (19:27).

On another occasion, having been treated to a picnic banquet the day before, people sought out Jesus, and the conversation turned to what it meant to believe in the Messiah (see John 6:29). Jesus spelled out the consequences to them in stark, radical language. This produced some grumbling among the local Jews, which continued in the local Capernaum synagogue and led to heated argument, resulting in many of his disciples saying, 'This is a hard teaching. Who can accept it?' (John 6:60). The fallout of all this was that, 'From this time many of his disciples turned back and no longer followed him' (John 6:66). When faced with the true cost of following Jesus, many decided not to do so. Jesus asked the small group of twelve, 'You do not want to leave too, do you?' (John 6:67). Simon Peter answered him, 'Lord, to whom shall we go? You have the words of eternal life' (John 6:68). Yet even in this small group of intimate friends, Jesus knew that there was one man who was still counting the cost. Judas decided that thirty pieces of silver was a better price.

We have read how Jesus taught among the Jewish scribes, the teachers of the law and the Pharisees, using parable and provocation. One night, one of those men from the ruling Jewish council sneaked into Jesus' room to pursue a deeper conversation, seeking answers to his uniquely personal questions, so that he might fully consider the cost of following Jesus. This man was caught up in the plot to trap Jesus, to try to terminate the pretensions of this upstart prophet from Nazareth. But we know that Nicodemus did decide to follow Jesus, as we read later how he took Jesus' body down from the cross and helped with the burial (John 19:38–42).

Each of these individuals made their decision about whether or not to follow Jesus in the context of a larger setting, having been part of a group of people around Jesus. The decision was made after being drawn into the accessible, yet deeply intriguing, dynamics of a new way of living that Jesus was introducing. We feel welcome in the company of these disciples because, like us, they are delightfully human. They talk openly of their failures, speak out of turn, get competitive and make impossible requests. They express their inner turmoil and also their longing for more of the life Jesus offers. We feel at ease in their company; we could belong to such a group.

Working late

How, then, do we each get into such a group, a community like this, and invite others along? On Wednesdays I cycle home, having finished work at the church at 5.30 pm. We eat as a family at six o'clock. I skip my duty as dish-washer and lie down on the sofa for five minutes. At 6.30 I return to church on my bike. The church lies just on the north side of the main railway line, heading east out of Tokyo city through dormitory towns all the way to Chiba city, an hour's ride away.

As I cycle under the four-track raised railway line, the train thunders past, already quite full, with people standing. Within a few minutes, I am at the church. The Japanese assistant pastor has taken even less time for his meal, is already at the church, and has put on the lights and heaters. I bring down the hymnbooks and songbooks from the church sanctuary upstairs and sneak a little piano practice before others arrive for the Wednesday evening midweek meeting.

I begin the meeting at seven o'clock with a retired university professor, Mr Sato (mentioned in the previous chapter), a younger man unable to work for health reasons and the assistant pastor. A retired businesswoman arrives at 7.10 and a Christian nurse at 7.20. Miss Ukiya, co-founder of the church, arrives at 7.30. As we sing, pray and study the Bible together, one or two more drop in. We stop at 8.30 and snack on rice crackers, buns filled with red bean paste and doughnuts, and drink green tea.

As Sozo and I cycle home together at nine o'clock, the trains heading out of Tokyo are noticeably fuller, bodies now firmly squeezed up against the doors. The number of commuters will not peak for another ninety minutes, with several thousand people per train every three to four minutes for another hour after that.

Most of the church members work during the day and do not arrive home until well after our meeting finishes. Those homes are thirty, forty or even fifty minutes away from the church. So midweek meetings are difficult to schedule, and our Wednesday evening meeting is therefore not a key opportunity to teach and train disciples. We do not hold any other weeknight evening meetings, even for young people or children, as no-one would be free to attend them and none of our members would be available to lead them. This is not only a Japanese problem. Anyone working in a large city, living an hour's commute from home, faces a similar struggle, especially with the economic downturn requiring a smaller number of employees to work longer, later hours. So what can we do instead?

Those who have time to attend groups that meet during the day can form an open community, such as the Ladies' Circle that Sachiko joined. For non-Christians who work on Sundays, this may be the only Christian community they could visit. But for people who work during the week, how can we provide a welcoming community, rather than just a meeting to attend? Working hours in the UK have lengthened over the last decade, and social patterns have adapted. Have you noticed that Christians no longer automatically make church the centre of their social life? Christian couples no longer spend three nights a week at church, attending midweek meetings and leading youth clubs. They enjoy social lives outside church, which can be highly fruitful. This is where we meet people, initiate friendships, establish trust and show our care for others. It is also the primary place where we debunk preconceptions about Christians. One consequence, though, is that it is more difficult to get people to attend a church meeting in the evenings and even more difficult to create opportunities for an open community. If, in your experience, church meetings are more difficult to find time for than they used to be, how much more so for not-yet-Christians who might consider attending? I think one solution is a re-envisioning of Sundays.

Sundays are special

The local church's largest gathering, usually the Sunday morning service, is a flagship event. It is also well wrapped up in 'our way of doing things' and resistant to the small changes that make it more open, inviting and accessible to friends and neighbours who are unfamiliar with church. Since our ten o'clock service includes twenty or thirty children, we try to keep the duration down to fifty minutes, but it usually goes a few minutes over. Afterwards, the kids rush off to their respective groups. Christians who are not involved in helping with the children's groups gather in a men's or women's group to share from the sermon and pray together. We invite any other visiting Christians to join the groups if they wish. Each group usually has one or two non-Christians in it. There is also a structured Bible study course for non-Christians who would like to know what the Christian faith is all about.

With all this activity, we have to keep an eye open for other newcomers who don't know where to go or how to fit in. It may mean standing with them for a few minutes of conversation before they leave, or inviting them to stay an extra quarter of an hour for a cup of tea downstairs.

We find that those who are most interested tend to stay on for lunch. This is usually a significant step for newcomers, when they feel that church is more than just a place where others perform religious rituals. It is also a place where, even as non-Christians, people are welcome to drink tea and share in conversations over lunch. Almost everything we do in a formal setting is initially unfamiliar to those without church backgrounds (more about this in the next chapter). We have found that, more than what they hear in sermons, it is the relaxed atmosphere, the freedom and the fun afterwards that settles newcomers' unease. Japanese society is highly stratified by age, so many newcomers are struck by the warm inter-action from those in their nineties down to the kids playing outside. We sing 'Happy Birthday' to each person born or baptized that month. It is often this family community atmos-phere that persuades people to return. This atmosphere of welcome and 'at-home-ness' eases their feelings of strange-ness and sets them free for deeper appreciation of the content of the worship services and the Christian life. I have to admit that it took me a while to unlock myself from my own rigid patterns of Sunday observance to appreciate the benefits of this approach. The church stays open for the rest of the afternoon as a place for rest and relaxation, chatting and praying, practising and preparing for future events. We do not hold an evening service. For three quarters of the people who come to the church on a Sunday, both Christian and non-Christian, it is the only time during the week that they can meet together in Christian community. For non-Christians, it is of crucial importance in forming a positive opinion of Christian community and the church of Christ.

Although some churches in the UK and across the used-to-be-Christian Western world have large numbers still attending evening services, attendance has largely dropped alarmingly. I have talked with quite a number of pastors who have asked, 'What should we do?' It is a matter of re-education and retraining in how to spend Sundays. One person asked me quite seriously, 'If there weren't an evening service, what would I do?' I think inviting Christian and non-Christian friends round for a meal or movie on a Sunday evening would be a great chance to do good to others, build trust and friendship, and enjoy community together. Of course, you can do these things on Saturdays or any other day you have free. Eating together is a biblical way of creating community. However, proactively using Sunday evenings for opening our homes to others, Christian and non-Christian, would be a pragmatic way of retraining our minds, bodies and schedules to a different way of making Sunday special, special for others.

Rebuilding programme

I hope I have aroused your interest in the benefits of unhurried community, particularly on Sundays, to which non-Christians feel welcome. After all, part of the church's uniqueness lies in the fact that it exists for non-members. Unfortunately, church is often seen as a group of people who rigidly attend a morning and evening service, with Sunday lunch in between. Occasionally, the church mounts aggressive scouting parties (if only they were parties!). We need to free ourselves from structures that are no longer helpful and capture a fresh dynamic of open community.

We all need to think through the unintended consequences of how we do church and how we spend time on Sundays. When I am in the UK, I have to be careful not to preach for too long, as it makes the congregation tense. I realize this may be only a British custom, but putting your Sunday lunch in the oven before attending church hampers your own schedule, as well as the preacher's. I admit that Sunday lunch is one of my great delights when in the UK, but the lack of open, vulnerable, authentic fellowship with other Christians in church on a Sunday is one of my greatest disappointments. In these days of microwavable meals and takeaways, we should be able to provide an easy lunch on Sundays. We can harness the simple dynamic of Mary, 'only one thing is needed' (Luke 10:42, which could also be translated 'only one dish is needed'), rather than our common prayer on Sundays: 'Give us our weekly banquet.'

Jesus was tough on the Pharisees for the rules they imposed on others. Jesus said the Sabbath day was made for us, not the other way round. Sunday remains the best day of the week for creating a community that opens its doors to all. We, the church, are not a unique community because we meet at 11 am and 6.30 pm on a Sunday. God has given us the day to richly enjoy worship and rest, on our own certainly, and with our families, but particularly in the larger congregational community – to worship together, rest together and find re-creation together, in noisy celebration or quiet reflection. The unique community of the church is best enjoyed when our structures allow others to join in as relaxed participants.

welcome. do you speak jargonese?

An invitation

She invited me to church at a barn dance: 'I'm a Christian. On Sundays I go to church. Would you like to come?' For no other reason than the opportunity to see her again, I agreed. I was eighteen, had never been to church before and had no idea what to expect. As I stepped inside the church the following Sunday, I was handed a hymn book, a song book, a prayer book, an order of service and a Bible. Somehow I reached an empty seat without dropping them. We stood, prayed, knelt, sat, sang. We read from the Bible – I couldn't find the passage. Everyone knew the spoken responses. I didn't. We even stood up to read – that was odd. I knew no-one, couldn't see the girl who invited me and didn't know what was coming next. Can you remember your first visit to a church? How did it feel?

In the chair again

The dentist held something between my teeth and told me to

bite, but I got it wrong. I had understood the word for 'bite' well enough, but didn't bite the way he wanted. The dentist repeated his instruction; it was the language children use, so it sounded just like its meaning – like the English words 'whoosh', 'whizz' and 'wham'. But not to me. On the fourth or fifth attempt, I figured it out and bit down solidly on to whatever it was between my teeth. The dentist had assumed that, because I spoke Japanese, I would understand every word he said. That is only true until I meet a word I don't know!

Like any other language, Japanese has specialized vocabulary. Where in English we have loan words, originally from Greek or Latin, for medical terms, Japanese uses Chinese character compound words. For vocabulary relating to computers or hamburgers, it uses many loan words from English. Even for native speakers of the language, discussion of an unfamiliar topic, such as politics or economics, flower arranging or *shogi* (Japanese chess), can leave the uninitiated struggling to keep up. I can talk to someone in Japanese with relative ease if the subject is sumo or origami, but I soon find myself floundering if the topic shifts to baseball or birds.

Even now after many years of going (or, in my case, trying to avoid going) to the dentist, I still encounter new words and phrases. I have just changed my dentist, and the new dental centre uses different phrases for many things, so I am hampered on a number of levels. First, of course, I am not a native speaker of the language. Secondly, I cannot see the dentist's lips because of the hygiene mask, so I find it hard to pick up the individual sounds. Thirdly, they speak too quickly for me to process the meaning. They use the same words and phrases hundreds of times a day, so they don't slow down. All the patients understand though, right? I find myself desperately trying to figure out the meaning of what they have just told me, while trying to keep my mouth open, not to swallow – and to relax my tense body. Once I have tracked my way through the forest of unfamiliar verbs and nouns and understood what they mean, I can appreciate that their explanations are well thought out and helpful to most patients. But as a first-timer to these explanations, as an inexperienced, linguistically challenged (albeit educated) person, I do not find them particularly user-friendly. I usually feel both stupid and hassled. As I leave, the dentist cheerily adds, 'See you on Sunday', with an aside to the dental nurse, 'He's my pastor.' In this chapter we are going to look at how we can offer a better welcome to those who are unfamiliar with church into the life of our congregation.

My first time at church

It was my first Sunday in the Chapel of Adoration. I sat through the service, wondering how I was going to remember the names of all these people with black hair and brown eyes. At the close of the service, I spoke falteringly to the man sitting quietly next to me. I had to start somewhere. 'So how long have you been coming to the church?' 'Today is my first time,' he replied nervously. I didn't admit to the embarrassed relief I felt. 'What made you come to church?' I added gently. 'My girlfriend invited me,' he explained shyly. I found that funnier than he realized – after all, I too had gone to church for the first time because of a girl.

A few months later, he joined the seekers' group I ran after the morning service. He was the first person I baptized. But on that first Sunday, all we knew was our shared fear of an unknown place and unfamiliar people.

On any given Sunday, we expect at least one if not two or three newcomers to church. While some are Christians invited by their friends, for as many as half such newcomers it will be their first ever time in a church. In addition to those who are brand new to a Christian worship service, there may be twenty or thirty others who are not yet Christians among the congregation of 120–140.

We are gentle with their unfamiliarity. When the leader of the service opens in prayer, we explain what we are about to do: 'I will pray. For those new to praying, please stand in an attitude of silent prayer.' The Japanese are accustomed to standing in silent prayer at Shinto shrines. We take care with our use of specialized language. An innocuous sentence such as 'We will praise God' can be highly confusing to first-time visitors to the church, if left unexplained. They will have never heard the verb 'to praise' before, and even knowing the two Chinese characters with which it is written does little to fill in the void of meaning. Moreover, there are 8 million gods in the Japanese pantheon, so we need to be a little more precise in our use of the word 'god' to avoid misunderstanding. So, for example, 'We will praise God with the words of hymn 208' becomes 'We will use the words of hymn 208 (in the black book in your pews) to express our thanks to the God who made everything.' Although not every phrase can be translated into first-time friendly phrases, we try to provide enough explanation so that inexperienced newcomers can understand and take part in the service.

Welcome mat or judo mat?

Our desire is to make the church a welcoming and unthreatening place. After all, the sermon is going to be hard to understand for those who have never read a Bible or heard of Abraham or Paul – especially if they attend on the thirtieth Sunday of a series on Genesis or Revelation. I don't expect the sermon to be the most attractive part of the service for someone attending church for the first time. We greet newcomers warmly as they arrive, do our best to help them during the service, either from the front in how we lead the service, or in person, by helping them look up Bible passages and checking they have picked up the correct song book. When the service finishes, we introduce each newcomer by name, as is the Japanese custom. They stand and bow. We welcome them with a brief, warm round of applause. Although it would also be customary for the newcomer to give a self-introduction, to explain who they are, where they are from, and even give their impressions of the church, we take the pressure off them. We do not want them to spend the worship service planning what they will say at the end. Instead, we invite everyone to stay for lunch afterwards, and if newcomers choose to stay, we give them a chance to introduce themselves there if they wish. We don't pressurize them to say they will come again next week.

I have attended smaller churches where half of the twenty or so members of the congregation surround a newcomer as soon as the service finishes and pepper them with personal questions, culminating in, 'Are you coming next week?' This approach may work in some cases, but will be off-putting to most visitors. Some want to slip away quietly after the service. As long as we have been attentive to them during the hour or so they have been with us, we do not chase them to stay longer. Others who have been brought by friends, or those wishing to linger, will be approached by those of similar age and interests, and longer conversations will hopefully ensue. Even then, a gentle 'Thank you for coming. Come back any time' as they leave is as strong as we get. If God sent them and we have welcomed them, God can make sure they will come again. The first day you come to church is a big step in a much longer process, a process that will have had many twists and turns along the way. In the following week, we usually send a postcard to thank them for coming.

The man who shared his first Sunday with me was from a Christian home, but he had kept well away from church. His girlfriend had been coming to the church on and off for a year or two, the relationship was getting more serious and she had encouraged him to attend church. I am glad we were gentle with him. He has become one of the key men in the church.

We are, after all, to be like fishermen. When we see a fish in the river, we don't jump in in our heavy boots and try to grab the fish and wrestle it from the water. Fishing is more subtle than that. When a person steps into a church for the first time, it is a crucial midway point in a God-governed process of establishing trust with the Christian community. We have to be careful that our overeagerness does not spoil the process.

What language did Jesus speak?

Paying attention to our use of language is a common courtesy in personal communication, cross-cultural or not. Jesus used different language when relating to various groups of people. In his clashes with the religious leaders of his day, he referred them to the Old Testament: 'Have you never read what David did when he and his companions were hungry and in need?' (Mark 2:25). He quoted the Jewish Scriptures to them: 'Isaiah was right when he prophesied about you hypocrites; as it is written . . . ' (Mark 7:6). He expected them to have a comprehensive understanding of the Old Testament: 'What did Moses command you?' (Mark 10:3). With religiously informed people, he used specifically religious terms, such as 'Sabbath' (Mark 3:4), 'Satan' (Mark 3:23), 'Holy Spirit' (Mark 3:29) and

'Corban' (Mark 7:11). When dealing with the rich young man, Jesus referred to the Ten Commandments, because he knew the man observed them closely (see Mark 10:17–22). For those who gathered in the courts of the temple to be taught, Jesus even quoted from the Psalms (Psalm 110; see Mark 12:36).

But for those who were less familiar with religious terminology, he used simple, everyday language. Jesus spoke to the country crowds about farmers sowing their annual crops and the mystery of plant germination and growth (Mark 4). Any householder would have understood the folly of lighting a wick lamp and covering it up: just as we would laugh at someone who unscrewed the light bulb before switching on the light. In conversation with a non-Jew, a Greek-born woman from Syria, Jesus talked, maybe even in Greek, about how you do not feed the family dog with food prepared for the children (Mark 7:27). The woman understood the figures of speech well enough to reply, using the same metaphor (7:28). Jesus' choice of theme and language made his teaching initially accessible to anyone, but it was never simplistic. The disciples were often intrigued enough by a parable to ask for it to be explained more fully.

Two stories in Mark's Gospel illustrate further the accessibility of Jesus' words. Jesus called Peter and Andrew, James and John, by saying, 'Come . . . and I will make you fishers of men' (Mark 1:17), not 'Come and I will make you apostles', although that was no doubt both his intent and desire. He used words handcrafted for these four men in that specific life situation. In chapter 9, he casts out an evil spirit. Amazingly, there is no jargon. Jesus asks the father of the possessed boy, 'How long has he been like this?' (9:21). Before a crowd could gather, he rebuked the evil spirit. ' "You deaf and mute spirit," he said, "I command you, come out of him and never enter him again" ' (9:25). This, if anywhere, is the sort of occasion that would be accompanied by special phrases, ritual and showy stuff. But the whole scene is described in normal speech, leaving the authenticity of the actions to speak for themselves, undecorated by religious verbal ornamentation.

Church-speak: Can you hear me?

We have spent a few chapters learning how to take uncertain steps into the cultures of the people around us. As we begin to respect the way others think, understand their values and walk alongside them in deepening friendship, we will establish a mutual trust. In time, we hope to see people approach the church through us (or others). We now need to learn how to help them as they encounter what may be to them a completely unfamiliar world.

After we have been Christians for a few years, the church feels like home and its jargon becomes familiar, even comforting. We forget how daunting it was when we first encountered it. Eighteen months after becoming a Christian, I was leading a Bible study with a fellow student who was interested in Christianity. After a while, she stopped me and asked, 'You keep talking about "the Scriptures"; what do you mean by that?' I had become overfamiliar with the jargon embarrassingly quickly. It was so obvious to me that I was referring to the Bible that I thought it required no explanation, but to this highly educated student who had grown up in the UK, my choice of words did not communicate what I thought they did. If I needed to be careful how I communicated in my own culture in the early 1980s, how much more scrupulous do we need to be these days, living in our globalized, multicultural contexts?

We long for people to come to church. When they arrive, we must welcome them gently, without confusing them unnecessarily. We must not presume they will understand all that is going on.

Can you imagine what it would be like for someone who had never been to a church before to visit your church next Sunday? I practised this one day in my local town. I was standing outside a Polish delicatessen, trying to summon up the courage to go in. The front window was a full-colour opaque picture of food, so I couldn't see anything inside. It took me two or three attempts before I pushed the door open. It looked like a small convenience store, but everything was in Polish. There were no other customers in the shop. An assistant was stacking shelves. I walked up and down the aisles of products with Polish names, feeling suddenly dislocated from my local high street. I felt bad just walking in and out, so I took a packet of 'papryka' costing 39p and nervously went to the counter, hoping the young woman would understand and that I would understand her. I was surprised how nerve-wracking the experience was. Try going somewhere unfamiliar and see for yourself how it feels. Go to a bird and wildlife centre if you know nothing about birds. Attend a meeting at a Jewish synagogue. Visit a Hindu festival. Try placing a bet at a bookmaker's.

If someone who had never been in a church and had never read a Bible came to your church on Sunday, what would they not understand? What would make them feel foreign, unsettled and unwelcome? The need for this awareness is not restricted to the preacher of the day and whoever is leading the service. The newcomer may sit next to you, may be a similar age to you, or live near you. You may be the most suitable person to welcome them and make them feel at home in this strange new world. Everyone can pray for such newcomers, and some can seek an opportunity to come alongside them and explain, gently, what the order of the service is all about. Could you explain the order of service without using Christian jargon? Much of what we do on a Sunday has become so ingrained that we may find it hard to explain to someone else. We should approach newcomers with humility and love, make them feel welcome and tell them that it is fine if they don't know what is going on. Our explanation is an act of caring for them and helping them to participate more fully in the overall flow of the service. We must be careful not to sound as if 'we know everything and you know nothing', otherwise we will further alienate the person we are trying to help. The litmus test for how well we welcome people is how relaxed and comfortable they feel being with us, despite not yet knowing what it means to worship God.

We need not dilute our language of all significant Christian meaning. However, we do need to be aware that our unthinking, unexplained use of language is likely to deafen others to the very message we want them to hear.

If you want to examine how welcoming your church appears to others, stare at your church notice boards for a while. Changing your notice board will not immediately result in people coming to your church, but seeing it through the eyes of others can be a useful tool in understanding how foreign your church may appear to newcomers. Ask yourself a few questions about it: How visual and how verbal is it? How colourful? What words would be unfamiliar to non-Christians? What words would be confusing – even antagonizing – to those from other religious backgrounds? What is the main thing that the notice board communicates? Will it be useful in reaching out to the people of your locality? How welcoming or inviting is it to someone who would like to step inside and see what is going on? Similar questions could be applied to the church website or leaflets. Do they exude an atmosphere of 'First-timers welcome'? Most Japanese do not think they have any right to enter a church because they are not Christians. I wonder if this is not now also the predominant view among people in the UK and other countries. Without clear signs and evidence to the contrary, the common view may well be that the church is a tightly huddled religious group and outsiders couldn't possibly intrude.

When staying in a bed and breakfast in Carlisle in the north of England, my son Daniel and I walked to a nearby convenience store to buy something to eat. On the way, my eye was drawn to a church notice board. In large letters it said, 'All welcome. Why not come along this Sunday? We love to welcome new people.' But it was the right-hand column that grabbed my attention:

Expect the . . . expected.

Church might be completely new to you – that's OK!
We'd love you to join us. We understand that trying anything new can be a daunting experience.

So here's what you can expect if you visit us on Sunday at 10 am:

We'll welcome you at the front door.

There will be a time of singing – usually around 5 songs (3–4 minutes each) throughout the meeting. You're welcome to sing along, or just listen in (the words will be provided).

There will be a time of prayer (again, you can just listen in as we pray).

There will be an update with church news and upcoming events.

A passage from the Bible will be read.

There will be a Bible talk (about 25 minutes in length). Children have their own 'Sunday Club' at this point.

We aim for our meetings to last about 75 minutes.

We serve tea and coffee afterwards. It's a great time to meet others.

We'd love to see you this weekend.

First-time tension

I often visit places in Japan for the first time: the City Office to fill in registration forms; an ENT hospital to be admitted as an outpatient; or a traditional Japanese soba noodle restaurant with a handwritten menu. I am usually greeted in one of two ways. As I step in through the door, I see the staff thinking, 'He's a foreigner; he doesn't understand; he can't speak Japanese, we don't speak English; help, what do we do? This is going to be embarrassing.' Then they welcome me with polite silence. They are unsure what to do, so they say nothing. The second response is to think the same things: 'He's a foreigner; he doesn't understand', and so on, and then ignore those factors completely and treat me the same way as they would any other Japanese person. It usually takes three or four visits before communication finds a middle road, as they come to realize that I can understand some but not all of what they say.

Similarly, in the church and in our conversations with non-Christians, we have to feel our way around what people know, and approach them appropriately. On a family holiday in western Scotland, we visited a church that was running special kids' events that week. But no-one came over and engaged our two teenage kids in conversation – not even one of the four Scripture Union workers who were in charge of the youth programme. It was a small gathering of maybe twenty people, informal and relaxed, yet no-one came and talked to my wife and me. At the close of the service over tea and biscuits, we approached church members to engage them in conversation! At another church in Antrim, where I slipped in unannounced, no-one knew me, but a man soon came over to sit with me and we talked for five or six minutes. He was warm and interested in me, and found out enough about me to know that I would settle well in the service. Afterwards, he introduced me to his wife and they expressed how glad they were that I had come, and that I would be welcome again any time.

The first time someone comes to your church is likely to be a small but brave step in a longer process of wanting to follow Jesus. Step into the newcomer's shoes; greet them warmly and gently. Anticipate, with faith, all that God may do in their life over the coming months.

9:

what do I say now?

Knock, knock

The first sermon I heard in my life was from Revelation. I had
no Christian background, and it was my first ever exposure to
a talk from a book of the Bible. Towards the end of the sermon,
the preacher, Michael Green, leaned over from the pulpit
and repeated Jesus' words: 'Here I am! I stand at the door and
knock' (Revelation 3:20). An almighty boom reverberated
through the church building. I was pinned to my seat.

It sounded again.

And again.

I had already been deeply struck by God's presence in the
church during the service. This almighty knocking was over-
whelming. At the close of the service, I prayed for the first
time. I prayed simply, along the lines of the preacher's encouragement that Jesus was inviting me back to a relationship with
the Father. I am convinced that I became a Christian that
morning. Much later, I found out that the booming sound had
been the bell of Christ Church, the college across the road,

striking midday. I had been a logical-minded atheist who had used clever arguments to deny God's existence and pour scorn on those who believed in God. It was God's felt presence and a sermon from Revelation that undid my hard heart – or maybe I was saved by the bell.

None of us knew, beforehand, what influences God would use to move us along through the process of conversion. We learned bit by bit how God was at work in our lives, leading us to trust and faith in Jesus' death and resurrection. The same is true as we accompany others on their journey to Jesus. We cannot presume to know exactly how God will work in their lives. With patience and the help of the Holy Spirit, we become more discerning of how God is at work in other people's hearts and lives, as he leads them to become Christians. It may not be like our own story, so we need to be ready with different approaches for different people.

Unknown journey

I was on the Tokyo Circle Line, heading for a station I had never been to before. Mr Sasaki was in the late stage of terminal cancer. His wife had asked me to visit him, with a warning to be careful, as he was quite anti-Christian. On this first visit, I talked gently with him, asked him about himself, and enquired if it was OK to pray for him and then did so. On the second visit, I read from the Bible and put my hand on him as I prayed. His wife told me later that he had experienced profound peace and comfort afterwards, and had asked if I would visit again.

Mr Sasaki had enjoyed a brilliant career in his own field. The disease progressed. During frequent periods in hospital over the following months, his antagonism to Christianity was replaced by a glad anticipation of my coming to talk and pray with him. I knew I was accompanying him during the final weeks and months of his life. His family and many in the church were praying for him to believe in Jesus. I talked to him about sin and God's judgment. I explained repentance and belief in Jesus, encouraging him to accept that Jesus had died for his sins on the cross. I was aware that he only dimly understood the underlying theology. What held him, and was good news to him, was the repeated sense of calm and peace each time I prayed with him. He expressed it as Jesus being with him. I had thought that, as a scientifically minded, highly logical person, he would most appreciate the clarity of my explanation of the gospel. But I realized that Jesus had reached his heart another way.

At Easter that year, after three baptisms at the church, Sozo the Japanese pastor and I went with his family to visit Mr Sasaki at his home. Although he was weak and hardly able to talk, we baptized him on his clear confession of faith in Jesus as his Saviour. His facial expression was filled with peace. He had not eaten for many days, but chose to celebrate with chocolate cake, which we ate together with great joy. He managed to finish off his own piece.

So what do you say?

After all our loving attention to establish trust with some-one, care and pray for them, introduce them to other Christian friends or a church small group, even invite them to attend church, when they reach the point of asking, 'So what's Christianity all about?' or 'What's the Bible?' or 'What does the word "sin" mean?', how do we answer their questions?

At university, in my first year as a Christian, I learned to give some answers to these sorts of questions. For example, the Bible is the infallible, inspired Word of God: 'All Scripture is God-breathed and is useful for teaching, rebuking, correcting and training in righteousness' (2 Timothy 3:16). Sin is our rebellion against God: 'For all have sinned and fall short of the glory of God' (Romans 3:23); 'For the wages of sin is death, but the gift of God is eternal life in Christ Jesus our Lord' (Romans 6:23).

I also had a number of tracts and leaflets to give to people. I was a young Christian, and this was a good way to start. However, I have found that this is a limited approach to explaining the gospel. It works well with those who share a similar view of the world; for those who believe in an almighty Creator and an absolute Truth, for those who respond to the force of rational argument and can accept the objective authority of religious writing. But in the UK and most other Western-minded countries, fewer and fewer people think like this.

As I was walking along one of the farm lanes near my home in rural Northern Ireland, I met a retired farmer. I explained that I had recently moved to the area, that I used to live in Japan and had worked as a missionary in the church there. We fell into easy conversation as he waited for his son to herd some sheep up the lane. Then he earnestly leaned in towards me and asked gravely, 'What are you trusting in for eternity?' To be honest, I greatly admired his urgency, passion and courage in asking me. But I was wryly amused that he felt he had to ask me that question, and with those words. He hadn't really understood where I was coming from – twenty years of preaching the gospel in Japan. He had only one approach to speaking about the gospel. We all have our own set of pet questions and answers, but we must assess their suitability before forcing them on others.

Mind the gap

There are two factors that force us to face up to this issue in our church life and in our community life. The first is globalization. Our main supporting church in Northern Ireland was completely Caucasian until a decade or so ago. Even those from England were no more than 1%. And yet, when I return to the area now, I see plenty of Indian, African and Asian faces when I walk along the street. I enjoy the chance to meet a Kenyan, Korean or Croatian Christian at church. One day I uncharacteristically wore a T-shirt and jeans to church, and just as the service began, a young man from Egypt sat next to me – dressed in jeans and a T-shirt!

As we reach out to friends and neighbours, workmates and visitors, we can expect our churches to show increasing ethnic diversity. But Africans have their own way of thinking. So do Latin Americans and Asians. I know how to relate to a Japanese person whom I might see in London, Oxford or Belfast. But I would not be so confident in how to relate to a Vietnamese person or someone from the Congo who I meet in Tokyo.

When I was invited to preach once in an international church in Tokyo, I found that half the congregation were Japanese, and the other half were a range of people from largely English-speaking home countries. I spoke in Japanese first, and translated for myself, paragraph by paragraph. I found the effort of preaching to two highly dissimilar groups hugely taxing, but not because of the language difference. I found it more difficult to preach in English to the English-speaking group. Although they shared a common language, their cultural backgrounds and experience of living in Japan were so varied, and my preparation had been with a Japanese audience in mind. It made me appreciate the enormity of the challenge for those who preach or worship in ethnically diverse congregations.

The second factor that affects the way we communicate is the ever-present chasm between generations within the same ethnic group. I have experienced the problem in my own church in Tokyo, where, for example, outmoded language in hymns and the use of traditional proverbs do not communicate with those younger than me. On the other hand, there are thousands of modern phrases borrowed from English that young people use, but the older members of the congregation often don't understand them. In many of our cultures, surely in all cultures, younger people and older people think differently. I would be highly frustrated if I were to have a conversation with myself as a twenty-year-old. Both of me would be frustrated!

There are many reasons why a younger generation thinks, communicates and processes information differently. Most are beyond the scope of this book, but two key factors are education and entertainment. My education involved learning from one textbook per subject, along with the teacher's input. My learning style was quite different from that of someone taught through internet research and group discussion. I grew up watching television programmes an hour long that now seem to move exceedingly slowly, even to my eyes. Those who have grown up on music videos and on-demand TV are less likely to be strong on sequential thinking and less enamoured by long presentations. The visual, multimedia approach presents numerous images, offers many thoughts in parallel, without the separate streams of thought necessarily being brought together or organized. Those unfamiliar with this approach may conceitedly dismiss it as not the best way to learn. I have had to learn, through my interaction with Japanese culture, that other cultures are quite often simply wired to learn differently.

As we see our churches welcoming people from other cultural backgrounds or from other faiths, we must be aware that our method of presenting the gospel should not be a 'one-size-fits-all' approach, but rather a 'one-style-fits-some-and-another-style-fits-others' approach. Whenever we read the Bible in any depth, we have to understand that Jesus spoke to people in their cultural context, usually first-century Jewish. We all understand the need for that. And we now need to be more aware of having to do the same for those around us. It affects what type of books we lend people (do we lend them a book?), how we write leaflets (should we use leaflets?), our church website design, our music, forms of hospitality, the style of our discipleship materials/programmes, the dynamics of our learning in small or large groups.

Choosing the right answer

So when you are asked, 'What is the Bible?', there are many shades of possible answer: the infallible Word of God; a collection of writings by Jews and Christians through which we believe God speaks to us; the story of Jesus coming to our world; a book full of hope. None of these answers is more correct than any other, but some may be more relevant to the searching behind someone's question, 'What is the Bible?'

If you were asked, 'What is the church?', you could give various answers: the gathered redeemed people of God across all ages; a family of brothers and sisters where everyone is welcome, equal and accepted. Even Jesus gave a variety of answers to the many who were asking the searching question, 'Who are you?' To the Samaritan multiple divorcee who said, 'I know that Messiah is coming', Jesus replied, 'I who speak to you am he' (John 4:25–26). To the Jews squabbling over the fact that Jesus healed someone on the Sabbath, he said he was the Son of God (John 5:16ff.). To the crowds of people looking for more miraculous food, Jesus said, 'I am the bread of life' (John 6:35). To the Jews who were arguing among themselves over that reply, he referred to himself as 'the Son of Man' (John 6:53). To Jews who said he was a demon-possessed Samaritan, Jesus stated, 'Before Abraham was born, I am' (John 8:58). He said to a blind man, 'I am the light of the world' (John 9:5). There are many more examples. None of these answers is comprehensive. But together they provide a rich and colourful tapestry of response to the question, 'Who is Jesus?'

Don't feel you must provide a fully comprehensive answer to a question. Most people who are interested in Christianity, the church or Jesus are picking up information and insight from a variety of sources. We each add our own colour and flavour, our own experience of God's goodness, love, care and salvation in our lives. But my own story and my explanation of the gospel, whether in a sermon, Bible study or conversation, will not, indeed cannot, be an exhaustive one.

From conversation to conversion

Each year the church holds a picnic. One Sunday afternoon, I was walking with a group on the way to the picnic site, twenty minutes from the church. As we approached the riverside, I turned to the young woman alongside me who I didn't know and casually asked, 'What do you do?' 'I'm a prostitute,' she replied. She didn't seem overly embarrassed by the admission. I struggled to keep the conversation going for the next few minutes. Of course, afterwards I thought of all the things I could have said. It was her first time at a church, and then she had stayed on for two or three hours for the picnic, talking with church members. I am fairly sure she was asking the question 'What is church?' But she wasn't looking for a wordy, intellectual answer. She had said she knew her life was a bit of a mess, and that she had questions about the way forward.

Much of life consists of conversation. The longer I live in Japan, and the more my Japanese improves, the more I am learning to listen to conversation. I listen to Japanese friends, newcomers to church, politicians and musicians, head teachers and doctors, teenagers and students, the lonely elderly and homeless people. I realize that most Japanese people do not think or speak the same way as I do. Back in the UK I find most non-Christians do not think like me either. Yet the agonizing human search for identity, belonging and meaning in life is common everywhere.

Japanese conversation is rarely open and direct. People deliberately hide clarity behind carefully hung curtains of ambiguity. I know that another Japanese person is able to stare at the shadows on the curtains and figure out fairly accurately what is behind them. Japanese culture trains and develops these traits of discernment. Conversations, even public speeches, do not tend to be formed along the lines of logic, deducing that since A is true and B is true, we must do C. Rather, meaning is associated with events and happenings, with people and relationships. I cannot change this, so I must go some way to adapting to it. It requires me to be involved in two-way conversation rather than one-way presentation. In our multicultural settings, including with younger generations, we need to make similar adaptations to our style of communication.

One year I chose to preach through Ecclesiastes, without skipping the sections I would rather have avoided. Christian scholars have struggled to find a framework to interpret this book of the Bible, but I found Japanese Christians and non-Christians appreciated the book with little help from me. Many commented, 'We don't really need your preaching, because Ecclesiastes is so much like our own literature; it speaks straight to us.'

Somehow, I found that encouraging. The style of the original text, its ambiguity and indirectness in not providing immediate answers but raising more questions, made it accessible to the Japanese. God spoke clearly to them through it.

Try reading Ecclesiastes with a non-Christian friend. Or better still, let them read it by themselves and talk about it afterwards. Don't rush them towards 'the conclusion of the matter: Fear God and keep his commandments, for this is the whole duty of man' (Ecclesiastes 12:13). Give your friends time to ponder, question, doubt and query the issues that arise as they read through it. Allow them to reach the conclusion in their own time. If you look carefully at Ecclesiastes 12:13, it doesn't expect anyone to jump straight to the conclusion. It says quite deliberately, 'Now all has been heard; here is the conclusion of the matter.' People need time and freedom to hear all there is in the book, without being herded to a conclusion they haven't reached yet.

Try a different approach

Mr Yoshida had been coming to church for a few months with his girlfriend. He was taking in the sermon content, reading the Bible for himself and attending my evangelistic beginners' Bible study after the service. On one occasion he asked, 'What does it mean to believe?' He wanted to know what you did when you 'believed'. I have heard this question many times. So when you believe, what do you actually do? I asked him to stand up with his back to me, and I took two steps away from him. I told him to fall backwards and I would catch him. It took a few false starts, but the conversation that took place during the course of the exercise proved to be a turning point for him and led to his baptism.

The Japanese, like many other Asian cultures, respond well to illustration, passion, emotion and personal anecdote. I have found UK congregations enjoy them too. When I first began preaching in Japan, my aim was simply to communicate the essential facts and doctrines of salvation history. That undoubtedly remains a vital part of the task, but there is more. The Holy Spirit has to use my words (whether in a sermon, Bible study or conversation) to reach beyond people's immediate thoughts and penetrate more deeply into their hearts and souls. So I have to speak out of an increasingly authentic and deepening relationship with Jesus himself, and communicate through illustration and story, passion and poetry, as well as abstract doctrine.

I was encouraged by a Japanese friend to write poetry. As a mathematics teacher, it seemed unlikely I would ever do it well. But I wrote a few Japanese short poems (haiku), reflecting on things I had seen. One was

みかんの木
場所いやがらず
実豊かに
A tangerine tree
not hating where it's planted
bearing much fruit.

The tree was growing in a 6-inch gap between a house and a concrete wall, and was exceptionally heavy with fruit. At the time, I was not enjoying my church ministry much. I have used that as an illustration for how God can bring hope and fruit from trying circumstances.

Since then, I have often written poems for myself in English, out of my own distress, sense of loss or betrayal. Many people live in difficult situations and are unable to express their agony, anger or sense of abandonment. Why not introduce them to the book of Psalms? The poetry and pain of the Psalms are less threatening, less direct than, say, Paul's letters, and often strike a deep note in people's hearts, without needing to press issues too hard. Don't analyse the Psalms for them. Poetry is easily spoilt by rushing in with explanations of 'what it really means'. Give them a chance to read it for themselves. Choose a few you think will fit their situations and allow God to speak to people through his Word in his way.

I wrote another haiku sitting by a paddy field on my day off.

人急ぎ
田を見張る鷺
立つ白さ
People hurrying
a heron guards the field
(out)standing white.

The heron had been standing completely stationary for fifteen minutes in the rice field, with cars hurtling along the roads on both sides. At the time, I was ridiculously busy and needed to give myself permission to stand still a while. I have used the haiku poem I wrote then to encourage people to be still, to try the biblical injunction, 'Be still, and know that I am God' (Psalm 46:10). In our 'if it feels right, it's OK' subjective culture, poetry can have a greater impact than carefully ordered prose. A poet strives to approach a common experience from a fresh perspective. Poetry is uniquely personal, while hinting at universal insight. You cannot argue whether it is right or wrong. Take a few friends and introduce them to biblical poetry.

My greatest surprise was how God spoke to people when I was preaching through Revelation. I certainly didn't start out on the book because I had already understood it. But as we listened to God's Word together, I found that they enjoyed the bold brush strokes of John as pastor, poet and theologian. They were thrilled, excited and encouraged by the new perspective they gained from this book of apocalyptic poetry. Their eyes were opened much wider, I think, than mine. 'Blessed is the one who reads the words of this prophecy, and blessed are those who hear it and take to heart what is written in it, because the time is near' (Revelation 1:3). We are all different; some are moved by logic, others by poetry. Some are inspired by story; others are stimulated by a parable.

Most of the people with whom we work, play or shop are not interested in finding out what is right, but rather what is 'right for me' just now. They may not be able to articulate it clearly, but they are looking for the appropriate, not the absolute. That's quite a Japanese way of thinking. If our conversation, communication and presentation of the gospel are limited to sucking a Bible passage dry for a few points of doctrinal truth, served up with well-connected logic, in order to tell people what we think they need to know, I suggest that, despite our sincerity, we are largely missing the opportunity to pass on the wonders of life with Jesus to our younger listeners or those with differing cultural backgrounds.

In a turned-off-to-Christianity UK, in order to create and maintain interest in what we have to say, we must tell more stories. Most of the Old Testament is story; the Hebrew people were great storytellers. I have found that human stories, particularly those of Abraham, Isaac, Joseph and others in the Genesis narrative, are a fruitful context in which

to discuss how God works in our lives, through our circumstances, mistakes and troubles. Preaching through Genesis
12 – 50 one year provoked open, vulnerable, transforming
conversation and prayer with non-Christians, who commented
how accessible they had found these authentic stories of real
people, messing up but seeking God, and God seeking them
anyway. Story is an acceptable medium in many cultures. The
Gospel writers tell wall-to-wall stories. They tell them well,
with huge impact. Many societies – Celtic culture, for example
– have a tradition of teaching mainly through story.

When we are asked what the gospel is all about, we can talk
about sin and salvation, heaven and hell, the cross and resurrection. But we must communicate those truths with the same
richness as the Bible does – with parable and poetry, story and
illustration, all of which will attract people in our twenty-first-
century culture, and are to be found throughout the Bible:
Psalms, Proverbs, Song of Songs, Job, Ecclesiastes, Genesis,
Jonah, the Gospel of Luke, Acts – even Revelation – all of God's
Word through which he speaks to those we meet.

10:

not-so-secret agents for mission

Waking up to opportunity

Mr Yamada crawls from his futon at 6.00 am, eats breakfast and leaves his house just before 7.00. He arrives at work sometime after 8.15, staring down the tunnel of another fifteen-hour day. His workload has been particularly heavy recently, as the insurance company he works for has undergone a merger. There are new office routines and staff changes. He used to leave work early on a Wednesday – much too early in his colleagues' opinion – so that he could be home by seven o'clock to eat a meal with his wife. But he gave that up in the hectic pre-merger period. His colleagues work on Saturdays and often on Sundays, but Mr Yamada takes Saturday to be with family and Sunday for church. However, to keep pace with his work commitments, he stays late at the office, arrives home around midnight, has a quick meal and then works until two or three o'clock in the morning before falling asleep. He lives his Christian life in the Japanese business world of stress, strain, compromise and exhaustion.

At weekends, he gives himself unstintingly to his family and church. For many years he led one of the Sunday school classes, he served a four-year term on the church leadership team and he still plays the guitar for the ten o'clock service every week. Although I used to work in a Japanese university, I understand little of the Japanese corporate world in which he works. I do not know how he maintains this pace of life, his health or his resolute, mature commitment to Jesus.

Although it may be an extreme example, his lifestyle displays elements common to many of us. Getting up early in the morning to commute to work. Having to work longer hours than we used to. Arriving home late. Not having enough time for family, friends and church. Living with higher levels of stress and fatigue. Wondering, 'Lord, should I give more time to church? How should I live out my Christian life at work?'

Mr Yamada's lifestyle is typical of thirty or so working men at the church, and maybe as many younger working women. Each Sunday they gather to worship Jesus and renew their desire to follow him. Many carry important roles in the life of the church, but their truly unique and world-changing contribution is not on Sundays. It is not principally at church. Their church is the community from which they are sent out to live in the world. They fully understand that they are the salt of the earth and the light in their company. They spend ten, twelve, fourteen, even sixteen hours a day, rubbing alongside their non-Christian colleagues. They want to shine into those lives, to somehow introduce them to Jesus. They are agents of mission in places I could never enter, in relationship with people I could never meet. God has intentionally placed each of us in our present life situations as agents in his mission to his world.

Having second thoughts

I had been leading the church for a few years. Having gained some pastoral experience and cultural understanding, I was trying to discern the way forward for the church as a whole. The church was started by a Japanese mother and daughter, who oversaw church life for twelve or thirteen years. Then it was given to OMF International, along with accompanying land. It was the largest gift in OMF history. OMF had looked after it for a similar length of time. I wanted to catch a glimpse of where we were going. For six months I met with the church leadership, six elected members, and we studied all the Bible passages regarding the purpose of the church. We reflected on the history of our church, reviewing all that God had done in miraculously intervening in the life of the founding Ukiya family, their construction of the present church building and the sustained growth of the church over thirty years. Combining biblical imagery with the living dynamics of the church as we experienced it, we distilled our essence as a church into a few lines. Translated into English, they run something like this:

> As those called out of darkness into his marvellous light,
> We walk in the light, becoming a church ablaze with light,
> That, as the light of the world, we may lead others to God's
>   light.

Our intention was not to produce a comprehensive statement regarding church, but rather to reach a deeper understanding of ourselves as a local church. This short sentence reminded us who we were, how we got where we were and what we were supposed to be doing. It sharpened our focus. However much we enjoyed our community life on Sundays and at midweek meetings, our focus was 'out there', not 'in here'. As a church, maybe you could take some time to review your own God-designed history. See if you can learn how God has used you and will use you as agents of mission in the future. This is especially necessary for churches that have been marginalized by twenty-first-century secular society. Many churches in the UK, across Europe and elsewhere used to be the centre of their communities, physically central to the town, city or village, and socially the hub of activity. They alone had large halls, and were spiritually the place where anyone in need went for help, guidance, support, care or comfort. In small towns, most people were 'churched', and the church's focus was appropriately on the many people in its care, probably most of the town. However, as many of our societies have turned away from Christianity and the Bible, the church has become physically marginalized. It is no longer the largest or most prominent building in town. It is thought socially outdated, quaint, even weird – most social activity happens elsewhere in town – and spiritually it is frequently viewed as irrelevant, hypocritical or old-fashioned, out of touch and just one option among many. For many churches, the need is to refocus their time and energy, passion, love and commitment from 'in here' to 'out there'.

Moving out

The same year as the above church review, I was preaching through Matthew 5, and when I reached verse 16, I had to teach what it means to 'let your light shine before men, that they may see your good deeds and praise your Father in heaven'. It wasn't a matter of teaching men like Mr Yamada how to behave in church, but how to live and do his job as a Christian.

As you go out of your door today and see people on the street, on the bus, at the desk next to you, how will you look at them? Where are they: in their relation to God, in relation to ourselves as Christians and in relation to the Christian church as a whole? Evangelism depends on seeing our friends, workmates and neighbours in a new light, perceiving the relationships around us with greater sensitivity, and relying on the Holy Spirit in the way we respond to them. With his help, we will enjoy not just a new way of looking at those around us, but also a new way of living in relationship with them.

As I was preaching through the Sermon on the Mount, I saw that Jesus didn't expound a strategy or method for evangelism. Rather, he gave a description of those involved. In the early Beatitudes, 'Blessed are the poor in spirit . . . the meek . . . the merciful . . . ' (Matthew 5:3–12), Jesus is describing the character and lifestyle of those who are 'the salt of the earth' and 'the light of the world' (Matthew 5:13–14).

The context in which Jesus was teaching these Beatitudes was one of mission. Jesus had called the first disciples to be fishers of men (Matthew 4:19), as we saw in the first chapter. This happened in Galilee of the Gentiles, an area with both Jewish and Gentile communities. Even at this early stage, the scene was being set for cross-cultural mission. Jesus healed many in the community and taught in the local synagogues. Peter and Andrew, James and John and their friends soon got the message that they were essential to their community, as essential as salt was for preserving their food all year round. Likewise, we are absolutely indispensable to the life of our communities. In these early chapters of Matthew's Gospel, we see how Jesus' lifestyle, expressed in word and deed, drew people towards God. Jesus does not pronounce the blessings of the Beatitudes as moral standards to live up to, but rather he offers them as practical examples of how we are to live together in community with God's blessing and so attract people to God and impact society. This is how we should seek to live around those who don't know Jesus.

God has chosen each one of us, like those first disciples, to be unique individuals in his kingdom community. The Beatitudes describe the various areas of our lives that God transforms by the working of his Holy Spirit, so that we can shine as we relate, in our actions and words, to others in human community. The blessedness mentioned is not a doctrinal ideal that we can never attain; it is a deep-seated well-being, experienced and expressed in our human relationships.

In Japanese society, where every nuance of language and gesture, of restraint and silence, is noted and analysed, Christians who live out these attitudes because Jesus is living within them will be quickly noticed, though not always with appreciation. Jesus was clear that at times our words and actions can, and indeed will, provoke persecution. In Japan, for example, many businesses hold Shinto ceremonies to ensure the company's success and prosperity, ceremonies which Christian employees, like everyone else, are expected to attend. Not going along with what everyone else is doing is considered unacceptably rude. Most weeks there are news reports of large- and small-scale financial mismanagement in companies across Japan. Christians working in those places may feel they need to speak up, even though they will be ostracized for doing so.

My own failed foray into the workplace in Japan (see chapter 5) earned me a silent ride home, and I was turned out of company housing into the street. However, my actions did precipitate a change in employment policy for all foreign staff at the school – not that I recommend my attitude or reaction on that occasion. Most importantly, as we live out our blessedness in human community, God is at work through our well-lived moments and is surprisingly unhampered by our bungled failures.

The crucial dynamic: God at work

I am convinced that God is at work in our world. I see him at work in two primary ways: he is at work in those of us who already know him, and he is also at work in others around us who do not yet know him. It is when these two arenas of God's activity overlap that we witness the exciting dynamic of mission.

First, the Holy Spirit is at work in you and in me. How we talk about this in our homes and churches may differ according to our Christian tradition, but the variety of our modes of expression does not alter the simple, glorious reality that God himself, in person, is at work – and at home – in our souls. When we praise God, the Holy Spirit of God leads us. When we pray, he guides us. When we wait in silence, he hovers over our hearts. When we listen to a friend's conversation, he gives us discernment. When we begin to speak, he gently moulds our words. When we bear with one another's faults, he trains our patience. When we are motivated by loving kindness to help someone, he purifies our hearts. He transforms our inner world of desire and motive, longing and aspiration, renewing our psychology and imagination which have been twisted by self and sin. He renews our reason and reckoning, by revealing to us all that Jesus said and did. Thus, our behaviour in word and deed, in other words our human relationships, is transformed by his love and light. We need to give our time and energy to his fruit-bearing activity within us.

Secondly, the Holy Spirit is already at work in the hearts of people who have not yet been drawn into God's kingdom.

Everybody we know lives with questions and doubts: Why do I find it so hard to get on with my boss? How can I find happiness? Why do I feel such despair? I so wish I hadn't done that! What's life all about? Why am I here? You can be sure everyone you know has inner uncertainties and hidden fears, although they may cover them up with busyness or bravado. Their consciences may be softening or hardening towards the inner dialogue, but it is here that God is surely at work, in their darkness, touching, probing and waiting. Through every news report or novel, each life situation and relationship struggle, each Christian they meet and church they pass on the street, God is at work in ways too subtle for us to imagine. Jesus said the Holy Spirit would 'convict the world of guilt in regard to sin and righteousness and judgment' (John 16:8).

When God, at work in me, brings me into contact with someone else in whom he is also at work, we have a truly exceptional and unique dynamic. Between Christians, we call this relational dynamic 'fellowship', but when it occurs between you and someone who is not yet a Christian, we have God-initiated mission. God has initiated the work in us, and is already at work in the other person, bringing the two together.

When you think of friends, workmates, family, neighbours or business associates, it may be that you are the first Christian they have known. How much are you praying that God will gradually open their hearts? Which of them have negative preconceptions of the church and of Christianity? What can you do to overcome those attitudes and develop trust? This may mean that you also need to trust them. Who needs particular love and care right now? Whom have you known the longest? They may be more open to an invitation to a meal in your home, to a small group or to church. Of course, they do not have conversations with you all the time about where they are spiritually, but can you sense where they are, and do you have a better idea of how you should respond to them? Can you discern the appropriate reaction in the changing dynamic of each developing friendship? It requires a listening heart – a heart that listens to them and to the Holy Spirit. As you continue with them on their personal journey, pray that God will be at work in them and that he will use you as you provide your own unique contribution to God's work in their life. You may be surprised at what God will do.

More surprises in store

If we can live such Jesus-centred, deeper lives among our workmates and friends, then we become agents of mission, in the ways outlined in earlier chapters, among those who are as yet far from God. We wait, hope, pray and believe that others will be drawn to God and the church through our witness. But even when someone comes into the church and becomes a Christian, our task is not complete. However wonderful this is, God has more in store for them. We must continue to wait and pray, model and teach, encourage and train these new just-become-Christians, so that they live as salt and light in their own life situations and attract others to Jesus.

Disciples making disciples

I waited ten years for it. No-one knew I was waiting for it. Then it happened, twice. Sakura had begun attending our church as a teenager, along with her Christian family. Through the Sunday school teenagers' group and then the student group, she became a Christian and requested baptism. I baptized her. She became deeply involved in her Christian student group in university, committed herself to helping in church and teaching in Sunday school with joy and enthusiasm. After graduation, in her first year of working in a bank, she invited a number of colleagues to the church. One of those friends began to attend regularly, showed an increasing desire to know Jesus and committed his life to following him. He was baptized that Christmas. He is the first person I know of who has become a Christian through someone I baptized. I was so excited to see a disciple making a disciple.

Then it happened a second time. Yuki was a shy and timid girl. Her attendance at church both before and after her baptism was sporadic. Often she wouldn't come at all for two or three months at a time. She would appear for a few weeks at Christmas, and then she would disappear again for months. Just when I honestly thought we had lost her, one day she brought her non-Christian boyfriend to church. After a few months of attending church together, she fell ill, but her boyfriend continued to come by himself, despite admitting to me that he was not searching for anything spiritually. Then his mother died, and he found out that she had wanted to become a Christian before she died. This made him begin his own search for Jesus. He became a Christian and was baptized that Easter. I was even more overjoyed, because in my (wrong) estimation, this seemed a highly unlikely route to be attracted to Jesus and come to trust him. But God makes his own disciples, in his own way, through the weakest and most unlikely of us, doesn't he? With a number of people receiving baptism each year, I thought the chances were reasonably good that I would see someone become a Christian through one of them, but I had to wait ten years to witness it. It is worth any amount of praying and waiting to see a new Christian lead another friend to Jesus.

The first piece of the puzzle

It doesn't matter where you are in your relationships with your friends or work colleagues. God is not hampered by where you are. He has put you there. I encourage you to start where you are. It is surprising what God can do through seemingly insignificant and inexperienced beginnings, as I mentioned in the first chapter.

Alison had only been out of Japanese language school a few months. We had just moved to the Tokyo area, with a four-month-old baby, to begin training in a Japanese church. A young Christian nurse who lived nearby began to drop in (rare in Japan) occasionally on Friday evenings. All she did was work on the jigsaw puzzle on the living room table and try to chat to Alison in English. We worked in that church for eighteen months, so she probably visited no more than ten or fifteen times. We thought nothing more of it and didn't mention it in our prayer letters, or see any deeper significance to it. She was an ordinary person from an ordinary background, and she felt God would not do anything significant through her. It turned out that we were the first missionaries she had ever met. Her overriding impression of us was that missionaries were simply ordinary people, like her!

Fired by this realization, she retrained as a midwife, and then applied to Bible college. On graduating from Bible college, she returned to work in Tokyo for a while as a nurse. Her new job was on the opposite side of Tokyo from her home and church. She decided to live in Ichikawa, since it was an easy commute to her new workplace, and after trying out a few other local churches, she became a member of the Chapel of Adoration. Over the following five years, we worked through the process of her becoming a missionary and being sent out from the church. She wanted to work as a nurse in an Asian country, in an area with poor health care, to be salt and light to the community. We never expected God to start anything like this when we were still being trained in language, culture and basic Japanese church life.

We said farewell to her at Narita International Airport, Tokyo, as she left for her country of service. After praying together, she gave her mother a final hug and walked towards the security gate. Suddenly, she stopped and began to panic, rummaging in her bag for her boarding pass. As a couple of friends rushed over to help, my eyes were drawn to a nearby sign. It had pictures of scissors, syringes and knives, with an instruction that sharp objects should not be taken on the plane. A brief English translation was provided underneath the Japanese: 'Voluntary Abandonment Please'.

I thought the phrase was an appropriate summary of what this woman was about to do: leaving her own country for another and setting aside her own plans to follow God's plan to work elsewhere, so that Jesus could work through her to reach others. At forty, she knew she would face extra difficulty in acquiring a new language and adapting to an unfamiliar culture. In her new country, she isn't allowed to preach the gospel, hand out tracts, or announce publicly that she is a Christian. She is restricted. But God is not.

After passing through the security gate, she emerged on the other side of the glass for one last time, before descending the steps to the departure gates. We waved from our viewing area. The last thing I saw was a Hitachi advertisement behind her. It can be summed up in English as 'Bringing you a better future'. I believe that is what each of our lives is about, as we abandon ourselves into God's hands and ask him to work in us, and through us to bring a better future to those around us.

I do not know how God will work through that ordinary nurse as she learns the local language and maybe does a jigsaw puzzle or two with people she hardly knows. I believe, pray and wait expectantly that he will, in his way and in his time, continue his remarkable work in and through her. I pray many will come to know Jesus. I believe and pray the same for you in your own unique situation. May God give us openness to the work of his Spirit in our own hearts, the passion to pray for others that God may work in their hearts, and the wisdom to see what our response should be when he chooses to combine the two in the world-shaking events of local mission.

Not-so-secret agents for mission

God has chosen you in Christ to be part of his exciting plan to gather untold millions of people into his kingdom. It happens here and now, every day, in your town, village or city. God continues to work out his plan and purposes through you.

Your problems and hang-ups, weaknesses and vulnerabilities, are where you will see God most at work in your life. They are the areas where you will relate most easily and authentically to the non-Christians around you.

Your experiences of God's love and care, help and support in the ups and downs of life, are so many little signposts that others need to see. God is at work today, in you and through you, reaching out in his abounding grace to your friends, family, neighbours and workmates.

You are one of God's not-so-secret agents in his mission to the world.

notes

1. Editorial, *Christianity* magazine (July 2011).
2. Melba Padilla Maggay, quoted without source reference in OMF Diaspora material.
3. Martin Goldsmith, *Matthew and Mission* (Paternoster, 2001), p. 63.
4. 'John, the Apostle', in I. H. Marshall, A. R. Millard, J. I. Packer and D. J. Wiseman (eds.), *New Bible Dictionary*, 2nd edn (IVP, 1982), p. 601.
5. Yuichi Hattori, 'Hikikomori: Japan's Hidden Epidemic', *Japan Harvest* (Winter 2008), p. 17.
6. Richard J. Foster, *Prayer: Finding the Heart's True Home* (HarperCollins, 1992), pp. 218–219.

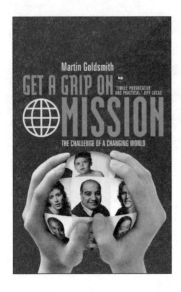

Get a Grip on Mission

The challenge of a changing world
Martin Goldsmith

ISBN: 9781844741267
208 pages, paperback

Globalization, pluralism, urbanization and increased mobility are just some of the challenges of twenty-first-century cross-cultural mission, and Martin Goldsmith helpfully equips us to respond wisely to them. With humour, confidence and enthusiasm, he enables us to see potential barriers to mission as opportunities waiting to be grasped.

The unchanging nature of Jesus' Great Commission contrasts strongly not only with our changing world but with our dynamic God. While his commands are set in stone, his methods are not.

This book will give you fresh ideas about mission. It will help you pray, plan and advise those who want to get involved.

'Valuable alike for doers, thinkers and teachers of mission.'
Revd Dr Christopher J. H. Wright

'Martin Goldsmith brings an impassioned heart and an informed, clear mind to this most vital subject. Timely, provocative and practical.' Jeff Lucas

Beyond Beards and Burqas

Connecting with Muslims
Martin Goldsmith

ISBN: 9781844744107
160 pages, paperback

Most people live or work among Muslim colleagues and neighbours, or mingle with Islamic people on trips overseas. But many Christians struggle to see beyond the stereotypes to connect in depth with the people they meet.

In this winsome book, Martin Goldsmith recounts colourful stories from a lifetime of conversations and friendships with Muslims in various countries around the world, including the UK. Part-travelogue, part-biography, readers are whisked from an English college garden to an Afghan market, from a London secondary school to a North African tourist destination, from Dubai airport to a home in Scotland, all the while becoming better equipped to make their own connections with Muslims – to the glory of God.

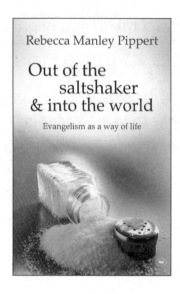

related titles from IVP

Out of the Saltshaker & into the World

Evangelism as a way of life

Rebecca Manley Pippert

ISBN: 9781844744282
292 pages, paperback

Evangelism isn't something you do, it's a world-changing way of life. Rebecca Manley Pippert shows how we as Christians, who are called to be the salt of the earth, can get out of the saltshaker and into life itself.

People crowd the pages, with language and lifestyles to match. She confronts them with a Jesus as contemporary as themselves, a Christ they can see, who cares. Reading her book we laugh at her mistakes, identify with her failures, and find ourselves eager to emulate her spiritual progress.

'This helped me to see that evangelism is a privilege rather than something you "wouldn't even do to your dog", as Rebecca Manley Pippert puts it so memorably.' Rico Tice

'A classic, and on a great theme. It introduces one of life's greatest joys: that of turning inconsequential chatter into speaking about Jesus. This is a must-read for all Christians.' Roger Carswell

Available from your local Christian bookshop or **www.thinkivp.com**